# The
# Old Testament
## in
## Contemporary
## Preaching

ONTARIO BIBLE COLLEGE

The Elmore Harris Series

*God and Evil*
*Encounter in the Non-Christian Era*
*The Old Testament in Contemporary Preaching*

# The Old Testament in Contemporary Preaching

Walter C. Kaiser, Jr.

BAKER BOOK HOUSE
Grand Rapids, Michigan

PHOTOLITHOPRINTED BY CUSHING - MALLOY, INC.
ANN ARBOR, MICHIGAN, UNITED STATES OF AMERICA
1973

*To our four gifts from God*

*Walter Christian III*
*Brian Addison*
*Kathleen Elise*
*Jonathan Kevan*

# Contents

# Foreword

The Bible, the Book of books, is a compilation of the sacred writings recognized by Christians as inspired by God and, therefore, of divine authority. The Old Testament contains thirty-nine books and the New Testament, twenty-seven, making a total of sixty-six in all.

Unfortunately, the Old Testament has been almost totally disregarded by the majority of professing Christians, who, of all people, should be eager to accept "the whole counsel of God." Perhaps the Old Testament meat is too strong. Or its commands may be too onerous. Possibly its prophecies are too obscure or too fantastic. Whatever the reason, comparatively few today would declare with the prophet Jeremiah, "Thy words were found, and I did eat them; and thy word was unto me the joy and rejoicing of my heart."

In our day, people are more inclined to read and assimilate the simple and more easily digested accounts of the life of Christ and the history of the early Church as recorded in the New Testament. The rugged brand of Old Testament religion is not for them, it would seem.

But Jesus Himself based His teaching on the Old Testament Scriptures. Likewise, the early Church, with its great protagonists such as Paul, Peter, John, and the others, had only the Old Testament as their foundation of revelation and truth. Indeed, many years were to pass before the New Testament would be completed and become a part of the canon of Scripture.

Accordingly, the Bible as a whole is the Word that God has promised to bless, and it must be accepted, believed in, and obeyed if one is to please the Lord.

We, at Ontario Bible College, have felt strongly constrained, through the Elmore Harris series of evangelical publications, to declare "the whole counsel of God." It is a great joy to be able to present the work of this edition by Walter C. Kaiser, Jr. as the third in the series. The author is a comparatively young man, but he has already made his mark as one of the world's outstanding evangelical Old Testament scholars. He is Associate Professor of Old Testament at Trinity Evangelical Divinity School in Deerfield, Illinois. We are indeed grateful to Trinity for sharing our brother for this most important undertaking.

These six messages originally were delivered by Mr. Kaiser as part of the Elmore Harris Academic Lecture Series and have since been prepared for publication by our own Douglas C. Percy, Director of Development at the college. We are confident that through them the Old Testament will come alive for many. It is our hope that Mr. Kaiser, with his keen insight, spiritual sensitivity, and his profound knowledge of Hebrew and countless other manuscripts, scrolls, and texts, will be used as God's instrument to set the joy bells ringing and to strengthen your faith. As for serious Bible students and readers, these pages will, as Spurgeon once said of another commentator, "set ideas wafting through your mind like sparrows twittering in a barn."

May this book lead you into a new and deeper study of the Old Testament and may the Old Testament prove to be for you a great spiritual asset, permeated as it is with its declaration of the Law of the Lord, its interpretation of history, its prophetic voice, and its wisdom of the ages. And, as Kaiser has so well pointed out, this indeed is the meaning of life with God.

STEWART L. BOEHMER
*President*
*Ontario Bible College*

# Introduction

So many different estimates have been placed on the Old Testament that it is difficult, if not well nigh impossible, to gather them all up into a single lectureship series and adequately treat them all. Therefore we have attempted to select some of the more obvious roadblocks currently found in evangelical circles.

Our evangelical disparagements of the Old Testament are mostly in the realm of practice and not theory. No one openly discards the whole Old Testament as did Schleiermacher; yet some evangelicals view this Testament as only a history of Israel's failures. Others elevate it to a slightly higher position, according it only the status of necessary background material for understanding the history of the New Testament. Still others go on to see in its pages scattered predictions of the coming Messiah, Jesus Christ. But alas, these references are not germane to its central message; neither were they even known or recognized to be Messianic predictions by those who first gave them.

Unsatisfied with the piecemeal results of the preceding estimates, still another view allegorizes all the Old Testament texts and receives a New Testament message in almost every Old Testament chapter. But this certainly "steals" the document from the hands of Israel and her Lord. The so-called "blessing" derived from this interpretive or allegorical method must not be equated or confused with divine approval for this almost cavalier treatment of the Word of God. Inspired the Word is, but a magical slate that can change its message and meaning with every new interpretation, it is not.

Then how should the Old Testament text be regarded? These six chapters argue for a progressive march of revelation, from the first words and deeds in Genesis, on into the New Testament. This march not only accumulates newer and fuller revelatory data, but it has an epigenetic* unity which relates the first truth of the Old

---

*"Produced by, not merely developed from."

Testament and the last truth of the New, even as a seed is related to the full-grown tree.

We believe we can identify that seed in these chapters. It is "the promise doctrine." Two of its main fruits can be identified also: "the Law and Wisdom." Hence, these chapters attempt to restore the confidence of the Christian Church in her Old Testament Scriptures. They seek to stimulate a more diligent search of the Scriptures, so that there may be a more complete, mature Body of Christ.

To sidestep answering any questions about the Church's relationship to the Old Testament is ultimately to court trouble in our corporate and individual spiritual lives. Our whole understanding of the Messianic person, the kingdom of God, the obedience of faith, the final work of God in history and with Israel, and much else besides, rests on our method of interpreting and regarding the Old Testament.

Therefore we seized upon the gracious invitation offered to us by Ontario Bible College and their Academic Lecture Series, to set forth some basic contributions on this topic. What appears on the following pages is the substance of three happy days, spent with the faculty, administration, and student body of that evangelical, conservative Bible College. The tone and content of the chapters is such that, while they are primarily addressed to serious, alert lay persons in the Church, they will also be of interest to scholars and professionals in the field. The tone is necessarily conversational and popular, though Douglas C. Percy, of Ontario Bible College, has given me immeasurable help by assisting me in preparing these chapters for publication, for which I am most appreciative.

Mention also should be made of those other unsung heroes who patiently transcribed and typed the manuscript in its multiple stages. Especially, I wish to thank Miss Marlene Williams, secretary to Mr. Percy.

Finally, to President Stewart L. Boehmer and his administrative staff; Prof. E. L. Simmonds, Chairman of the Department of Biblical Studies; the faculty; and a most generous student body, my sincere thanks and praise to God for our time spent together.

WALTER C. KAISER, JR.

*Associate Professor of Old Testament*
*Trinity Evangelical Divinity School*
*Deerfield, Illinois*

# 1

# The Old Testament

## The Christian's Asset or Liability?

The Old Testament: Is it an asset or a liability to the Christian? Or to paraphrase the question, "Why bother with the Old Testament?" This is a question often asked today, despite the fact that if we did not bother with the Old Testament, two thirds of the Bible would disappear. The Christian would be impoverished not only spiritually but also intellectually and aesthetically, since some of the greatest literature in the world would be lost. What must be done, is to investigate the function of the Old Testament and to see its value for the Christian.

It used to be said that heresy, historical criticism, and hermeneutics really were the greatest hindrances to enjoying the Old Testament. But they are no longer the sole competitors for one's attention. An even greater problem is the presence of sheer apathy, the alarming increase in Biblical ignorance, and the fantastic abuse of Scripture by means of spiritualizing the text. And I want to do battle, simultaneously, with all of these, if I can.

First, it is necessary to have an historical perspective if we are not to repeat the errors of the past. If we look at this history we will find an array of names of many distinguished scholars who looked at the Old Testament, sometimes superficially and sometimes in depth, and then passed their personal judgment on it.

Take the matter of heresy in history. Just when the Christian Church got under way, there was a second-century scholar by the name of Marcion of Pontus. He was a convert to Christianity, and he naturally began reading the Old Testament. I don't know what part he began to read. It may have been the "begats" of Chronicles or some of the other somewhat tedious references that have their value but are often repetitive. At any rate, he became bored with the Old Testament, and he decided that it wasn't for him. It is true that Gnosticism was in the air at that time. The God of the Old Testament was thought to be a "demiurge" and a "wrathful Deity," altogether different from the New Testament God of love. And perhaps if those were the only options, one can scarcely blame him for choosing the God of love.

I say *if* those were the only options. Marcion thought they were. So he began making a hard and fast contrast between *Law* in the Old Testament, and *Gospel* in the New Testament. Wrath, he said, characterizes the God of the Old Testament. Grace and love are the trademarks of the God of the New Testament. And "never the twain shall meet." Or so he said.

One thing is noticeable about Marcion. He had enough understanding and insight to realize that if he threw out the Old Testament (which he eventually did, laying aside two-thirds of the Bible), there were also implications for the New Testament. So he went carefully through the New Testament, taking things out that shared the same viewpoint as the Old Testament. The result was that he quickly reduced the New Testament, too. This left him with a narrow, inadequate book, comprised essentially of his reworked letters of Paul.

And then, as often happens, even some things that Paul wrote offended him, largely because they were the same ideas that are in the Old Testament. They had far-reaching implications. And so did Marcion theology. We might do well to go back and reread Marcion and see what happened to him.

Thus was the Marcionite pattern. He had some good questions. It's too bad that there weren't also good and able Christians there to answer them at the time. But the Church was young. She had her own problems. The Church was involved in the work of evangelism, and often the vital matters of discipling and following up with full teaching were not carried on. It is true that a few years later Tertullian wrote a tract against Marcion. But it's kind of hard, once a man puts his views into writing, to retract them. And Marcion had put his on the line. So he hardened himself and clung to his position; thus we have the continuing Marcionite tradition that is still evident in theology today.

Then there is the matter of hermeneutics. Hermeneutics is basically "the science of interpreting the Scriptures," a study that can either impoverish or enrich our Bible knowledge.

Toward the end of the nineteenth century, a bishop named John William Colenso illustrated this. Colenso actually was a brilliant mathematician who studied at Cambridge, and when he finished his work, he decided to go into theology. He did, and he became involved in the pastoral ministry and rose quickly in the ranks within the pastorate. But he had tremendous difficulty understanding eternal damnation in the Law.

There was quite a struggle going on in England in that day, much like the smoldering issues that lie just below the surface of theology today. Colenso, with the courage of his convictions, wrote a commentary on the Book of Romans. Unfortunately, for all his brilliance he could not master his subject. He couldn't believe that God would forever cast men out of His presence. But he had nothing to say about the possibility that man himself might really want to be apart from God. For there are some men who say, "God, get off my back. I want nothing to do with You." But all men, as Scripture teaches, live forever. Only some men must forever live apart from God, if that is their personal choice.

That is perhaps the "bad news" of the gospel. Nonetheless, God never annihilates anyone. It is a man's own choice—in spite of the many years when God chased him with His goodness and with His grace.

The Church quickly got Colenso out of England and sent him to the Zulus in Natal, where he became a bishop, a very high and prestigious office that was created for him. Then he really began studying the whole problem of the Old Testament. While there, he had the very high ambition of translating the Bible into the Zulu tongue. In doing this he used Zulus as his informants, and they began to ask him questions like, "Was that really true? Did Moses really say that slaves could be beaten with a rod and regarded as their master's money?" Bishop Colenso swallowed a bit and said, "Yes, it's all true." And all the while within his own mind he had his own large question marks. They began gnawing at him, increasing his difficulty.

Then while he was translating the Book of Exodus, chapter 21 —about the laws concerning slaves—the Zulus asked, "Is this the kind of God you have come to tell us about?" So Colenso wrote a letter back to his friends in England and to some of his professors. But he never sent the letter off. Things had moved too rapidly. By 1862, he had finished writing five mammoth volumes on the first six books of the Bible, entitled *The Pentateuch and the Book of Joshua, Critically Examined.* He tested and turned every little verse and word that he could, to show how one thing after another was wrong with the Old Testament, and why he could not believe it.

Colenso kept insisting that the whole thing was a fraud, and though the Old Testament really proved that the God depicted there was not an ethical God at all, he still thought it might have value for the Christian. How he could do so, it is impossible to conjecture. Evidently he made the error of using his own science of interpretation, his own system of hermeneutics. He thought he had the key, and by using his own unsanctified imagination, he came up with his own conclusions and his own answers. Unfortunately they are still with us to this day.

Since 1930, there has been a fresh, exciting rethinking of our theology in this area. This does not mean that we now have the answer for every "jot and tittle" question that anyone ever thought of. But there is information now available that would have silenced Colenso. He could have had tremendously solid reaffirmation for the Old Testament if only he had some of this material. Methodologically, he did not even use the material that was available in his own day.

The third charge is that of historical criticism. This has been batted around for a number of years. But about the time that Colenso was at the height of his battle, and really had England in a furor because of his position, another man arose in Germany. He was Julius Wellhausen, a youth of nineteen years. Since he was unaffected by almost all his professors at the university except an Old Testament lecturer named Heinrich Ewald, he decided to major in that field. So Wellhausen got involved in Old Testament studies. Nine years later—at the early age of twenty-eight—he was in a chair at one of the major universities in Germany; and shortly after that he began spinning out his own theory on the Old Testament.

He felt, as he tells us in the preface to his *Prolegomena to the History of Israel* (1883), that David, Ahab, Elijah, and other Old Testament figures were not fulfilling the Law, in his estimation at least. For he did not detect any references in the Old Testament Prophets or Historical Books to sacrifices being carried back to Jerusalem. He wondered why it was. The Law was supposed to have been given to Moses around 1400 B.C. But where he was reading of Israel's kings and prophets of a much later era, they seemed to have overlooked their own religious roots. Why were they not going back to Jerusalem to fulfill the Law? Wellhausen thought he had a good question.

One day, in a conversation with a famous theologian named Albrecht Ritschl, it was suggested to him that someone had proposed a theory that the first books of Moses really did not come before the time of David. They were actually written long after David's time, perhaps around 850 down to 400 B.C. This seemed to answer Wellhausen's dilemma. This prompted his theory that Moses did not write the first five books of the Old Testament; that rather, it was a composite work written from the ninth to the fifth century B.C. in four different documents.

All this started the famous documentary theory: J.E.D.P. This J.E.D.P. theory, standing for certain documents, became a whole new way of looking at the Pentateuch. The entire study of historical criticism, which started with the small beginning given it by Jean Astruc in 1753, came to its climax in Julius Wellhausen. Now it is the dominant theme in practically all the university courses being offered in the Western Hemisphere on both the Old Testament itself and on the religion of the Old Testament.

These now are up for definite reinvestigation. But they are open for reinvestigation not on the basis that we would naturally think of first—that is, on a view of Scripture as the verbal, plenary, inspired, and inerrant Word of God. This is true, but it has force only for Christians who are already committed. What about the man who uses historiographical materials, but also wants to use the tools of criticism and feels this is legitimate? Is he right? Yes. There is a legitimacy to this. But he should not covertly introduce or blatantly interject his distinctive philosophical *a priori,* and attribute this philosophical position to the writers of Scripture.

Within our evangelical circles, this type of destructive criticism that cuts the Pentateuch link now can be totally reversed. The very same historiographic and literary tools are shared by evangelicals, but without the crippling imposition of assumptions upon the writers of Scripture.

The key to the Wellhausean problem is the Book of Deuteronomy. The best answer I know is found in the book, *The Treaty of the Great King,* by Meredith Kline.[1] The first fifty pages of that

---

1. Meredith Kline, *The Treaty of the Great King* (Grand Rapids: Eerdmans Publishing Co., 1963).

book contain the most exciting news that has come out of the 1960s. The article, first published in 1960 and put in book form in 1963, is so cogent that to this day it has not received one critical review by a liberal journal. Nor will it. It is a beautiful response, and it uses the same procedures and the same methodology. We can be grateful to God and to His servant for such a searching reply. More about this will be covered later. But we can see that the Church faced at least three major attacks as represented by Marcion, Colenso, and Wellhausen. The effects of those challenges still exist for contemporary readers of the Old Testament. That is all history. What about our contemporary problem in the matter of apathy, which exists in evangelical circles, not to mention the large amount of Biblical ignorance? Try a Bible quiz on the average church group. They likely will identify obvious central characters and events in the Old and New Testaments. But move away from some of the central characters and there will be trouble.

But let us look more closely at the Old Testament. To be sure, people today can't get very excited about a book dealing with the Jews and their problems. It is a book for the Jews, about the Jews, and what they did to get out of the trouble in which they found themselves. Actually, their efforts seemed to inevitably lead to more trouble. Even the last book of the Old Testament, the Book of Malachi, shows that they are still in trouble. Why then should we read about it? Isn't it a book addressed just to the Jews? Why should we care? But if we love only "mythical" Jews (i.e., ones that exist in some sort of nonterrestrial, Biblical sphere), is this not dishonest since there are real Jews today who need to be loved and to become complete in Christ? We *must* care.

Furthermore, the Old Testament is not a book that preaches that God has "pets" or that He has favorites in His program as far as salvation is concerned. This is the number one thing we must put a torch to. We must end that theory. The Bible itself is against that point of view. If it is said that God has favorites as far as revelation is concerned, we can agree. The Bible teaches that. Read Romans 3:1-2: "What advantage then hath the Jew? . . . Much." But don't leave it there. There is much more, and this is what the Old Testament is really teaching. "Unto them were committed the oracles of God," the Word of God. But that Word of God was for others too.

The Jews were favored with one thing—the revelation. They heard the words from God's lips and passed them on to us. But what about salvation? Was salvation a closed club for God's chosen people until Christ came? What about all those non-Jewish people who lived way back then? How should we answer the question that for all those years and millennia God did nothing from the time of Abraham all the way down to the time of Christ? I can't believe that. And it's something I can't believe because the text does not teach it. I hold my finger on the Scriptures (I'm almost a biblicist in a right way) and I keep looking at the text. I look at Melchizedek, Priest of Salem (Jerusalem) (Gen. 14); and at Jethro, Priest of Midian, who was a believer in the Lord and who worshiped God and presented a sacrifice to be offered to Him (Exod. 19). Did God ignore them?

We are also impressed by Eliezer, Abraham's servant (Gen. 15); or by Zipporah, Moses' wife, daughter of Jethro (Exod. 4). Then there is Rahab, one who was not exactly the nicest type of girl. Yet she is called a "woman of faith." That's in Hebrews 11:31. So there is New Testament evidence that confirms this same line of argumentation found in the Old Testament.

At this point, however, some will complain about the primitive ethics of the Old Testament. For example, look at Rahab. Did she do right when she lied about the spies? Does the Old Testament condone lying? No, it does not. But it does approve one main quality in her life—her faith. This faith is seen in the fact that she feared the God of Israel more than she feared her own king in Jericho. That is what the text says, and it is found in Joshua. Read it and rejoice in a merciful, loving God![2]

I am impressed also by another non-Israelite entry to the Old Testament gallery of all-time greats: Ruth, the Moabitess. She was also in the line of David. Then there is a whole book addressed to people who were outside of Jewry. A whole non-Jewish city got converted at one time! Someone named Jonah went there

---

2. For an excellent discussion on this topic and other examples like it, see William Brenton Greene, Jr., "The Ethics of the Old Testament" in *Classical Evangelical Essays in Old Testament Interpretation*, ed, Walter C. Kaiser, Jr. (Grand Rapids: Baker Book House, 1972), pp. 207-35.

to preach. Not that he loved Nineveh or its people. Doubtless he said, "Why should I convert our number one enemy?" He knew what was going to happen. He knew that if he told them that after forty days and forty nights it would be all over, they might repent. And he knew that a loving, gracious God would show mercy if they did repent. Was Jonah afraid that it would reflect on his preacher status? And what about the Jews who still refused to repent regardless of any number of appeals? Jonah did not care to bring that type of message to any Gentiles. Therefore he had to be brought back by special delivery. But God was gracious; therefore His mercy was felt even by this Gentile city.

By the way, do you know that one hundred years later there was a sequel to the Book of Jonah? It is the Book of Nahum. There the same city and the same capital of Assyria was again visited by another prophetic word—this time, Nahum's. The Ninevites were addressed once again. But did they remember the lesson they had learned in Jonah's time? Not at all. So Nahum told them that judgment was coming, and this time it came.

There are more instructions in the Bible that are addressed to nations other than Israel. Read the eleven chapters in Isaiah (13–23). In Ezekiel are eight more chapters (25–32), and six more in Jeremiah (46–51). That makes a total of twenty-five chapters whose message concerns God's judgment and/or salvation of non-Israelite nations. Amos 1 and 2; Daniel 2–7; and Obadiah are other examples of this same universal scope of the Old Testament message. Why are all these messages in the Old Testament directed to men who are non-Jews, calling upon them to repent? Because—if the message is good for Jews, it also is good for non-Jews. As a matter of fact, God had already told Abraham, in Genesis 12:3, that "in thee shall all families of the earth be blessed." And that, says Paul in Galatians 3:8, is the "good news" that we preach. God says that the news that He gave to Abraham is the "gospel," or, as we say, the "good spiel," which we have shortened to "gospel," the good message, the good news that tells us we can have reconciliation with God.

To move on to the second objection, some complain about the Old Testament, saying that we should spend our time where we can best profit—to receive instructions on how to obtain salvation and where we can get good doctrine or spiritual rebuke and correction. Most, unfortunately, immediately conclude that this limits the scope of our study to the New Testament Scriptures. That is not what Paul wrote in II Timothy 3:15-17. There Paul is instructing a young pastor who has a Bible that has thirty-nine books. Together they go from Genesis through Malachi (in our present arrangement of the books). And he says to this pastor, "And that from a child thou hast known the holy scriptures, which are able to make thee wise unto salvation through faith which is in Christ Jesus."

Paul speaks only of the Scriptures that were already written, for the New Testament had not yet been completed. Did he not say that the Old Testament "is able to make you wise unto salvation?" That is exactly what the Bible teaches. Who ever got saved through the Old Testament? There must have been some, because the text says that we are able to receive salvation from the good news given in those thirty-nine books. Do you believe that? God teaches it! Believe it because God says so! Furthermore, for millennia that is precisely what happened before the Christian era.

Paul goes on to say, "All scripture is given by inspiration of God" (II Tim. 3:16). We have accepted that part of the verse, but perhaps we have forgotten the other part, which states that it "is profitable." Do not forget that what was written up to the time of Paul's writing was only Genesis through Malachi. And what is it good for? What is it profitable for? "For doctrine!" There are doctrines that come out of the Old Testament. "For reproof." That is also found in the Old Testament. Some say that they can get it better from Philippians or from Ephesians and Corinthians. This is true, but it is not limited to these books. The entire Bible is needed for the whole man: ". . . for reproof, for correction, for instruction in righteousness *that the man of God may be perfect, thoroughly furnished unto all good works*" (italics mine). Paul in effect says to Timothy, "That is just what the Old Testament was intended to do. It is intended to show us the Christ and to help us in knowing how to live—reproving us, correcting us, and giving us instruction in righteousness." Perhaps we should read, or reread the Old Testament sometime. If it is supposed to do all that, we should experience it for ourselves.

Perhaps we "believe" it because it is "in the Bible." But I wonder if we have ever looked at the Old Testament from this singular point of view; or do we regard it mainly as the preface or the prologue to the New Testament in which we believe we really get the reproof, the instruction, the correction, the righteousness, and where the man of God becomes thoroughly equipped to do that complete job?

We are using the Old Testament text here. But some may object and say that there is no gospel in the Old Testament. They want "Good News for Modern Man," not the Law. But look at Hebrews 3:16–4:2. Did you know that the gospel was preached to people in the wilderness? The text says so. The passage in Hebrews says,

> For some, when they had heard, did provoke: howbeit not all that came out of Egypt by Moses. But with whom was he grieved forty years? was it not with them that had sinned, whose carcases fell in the wilderness? And to whom sware he that they should not enter into his rest, but to them that believed not? So we see that they could not enter in because of unbelief. Let us therefore fear, lest, a promise being left us of entering into his rest, any of you should seem to come short of it. For unto us was the gospel preached as well as unto them. . . .

Who are the "them"? Are they not the Israelites who died in the wilderness? Do you see the antecedent there? There is a chapter division now, but perhaps in reading chapter 4, we have forgotten that only since A.D. 1400 have there been chapter divisions. Prior to that time, the message went on to say, "Let us therefore fear. . . . For unto us was the gospel preached, as well as unto them. . . .

Abraham also had the gospel. Turn to Galatians 3:8, where Paul makes the same point: ". . . the scripture, foreseeing that God would justify the heathen through faith, preached before the gospel unto Abraham [or pre-evangelized Abraham] saying, In thee shall all nations be blessed." That is what Paul teaches us. The gospel was preached to Abraham. This is what the text says. And we do well to receive it and teach that the gospel was available not only for an Abraham but for a whole generation of Israelites, and many others besides.

Romans 4:3-6 is just one more instance of the same truth. It says very plainly that Abraham and David were examples of men who were justified by faith. Abraham was a justified man, I'm a justified man; both of us stand before God on the same basis. What is that basis? The work of Christ. Without the work of Christ I would have no status, no standing, no end. But I do have status. I have an end. I am declared just before God. Because of what I did? Oh no! Because of what Christ did. And Abraham has the same position. Look at verse 3: "For what saith the scripture? Abraham believed God, and it was counted unto him for righteousness." And the text goes on in the latter part of the chapter to give the same point of view in regard to David.

Perhaps you say, "All right, I agree, there is a gospel there. But I do not see any grace." Let me point out one of the most beautiful words in the Old Testament—the Hebrew word *hesed*. The *hesed* of God occurs 250 times in the Old Testament. Where it is not used exclusively "of God," it certainly reflects His work. It is generally translated in the King James Version as "loving kindness," as in the psalmist's repeated refrain, "For His loving kindness [*hesed*] endureth forever." That is the "gifty" word in the Old Testament, the "grace" word. I like to speak of it as the "giftiness of God," since modern man doesn't know exactly what we mean by the "grace of God." It is the handing out of His free gift by the sheer act of His love on account of nothing that we have done, but only on account of His own bountifulness and love. And so God's grace appears scores of times in the Old Testament. It is actually one of the most difficult words to translate into one English word.

When the Revised Standard Version translation was made, they translated the rest of the whole Bible before making a final decision on this one word in its 250 occurrences. It was the last decision that the committee made. They finally settled on something like "steadfast love," because it spoke of the loyal love of God to His covenantal promise. I still don't know of one word or several words that can bring it across.

In addition to this word *hesed* there are other words like "love" that point in the direction of the Old Testament idea of grace. The idea of grace, in the opinion of some, more than any other idea in the two Testaments, is the one that binds the Bible together as a whole. For the Bible in its entirety is a story of the continuing work of the same God, how in His love and His "giftiness" He gives to man, when man has nothing to give back except a response of acceptance. Man can only say to such a God, "I take, I believe."

There is a further objection that some make. They say that we were not there in the Old Testament period. Therefore it is not addressed to us at all. The Old Testament is historically dated, and so they do not think they should accept it today. This is true, but we must make the point that *both* Testaments are historically dated. For example, when I go on vacation, I do not deliberately get into a boat and say that I do so because my Lord once said in the New Testament, "Get into the boat." It's Biblical all right. It occurs in the text. But it was a specific command to the disciples in a specific situation only. Nor have I ever gone out roaming through the countryside and, on passing a farm and noticing a colt tied up, go up to the colt and untie it because I remembered a New Testament verse that I read that morning, "Loose the colt."

Now these are not problems to you. These things are very well understood. But what about the word that comes at the end of some of Paul's letters, "Greet the brethren with a holy kiss." Nowadays, most people put their hand out, and try to fulfill the command that way. Is it insulting to the Biblical text? I do not think so. It is a matter of understanding the cultural context of the Bible.

Since we have that much common sense in dealing with such New Testament problems, why not treat the Old Testament in the same manner? There are some statements where the Bible is clearly intending only to offer a report. It is not teaching in those instances. Perhaps the most extreme illustration that comes to me was the time when I tried to counsel a man who was living in an incestuous relationship with his two daughters. He claimed it was Biblical. I have never argued with a man who had such a wooden mentality. I said, "But the Bible speaks against this." "No, no," he said, "it doesn't speak against it. It's Biblical." So I said, "Where do you find the Bible verse for it?" He said, "Lot lived with his two daughters." I said, "Yes, but God didn't approve of it." "Well," he said, "show me the verse where it says Lot was wrong." And you know, there isn't a verse that says, "Lot was wrong."

Oftentimes, the Bible assumes you have enough intelligence to know the difference between what the Bible reports and what it teaches. The Bible says, "There is no God," but it only reports that "the fool says so." It's possible to form a trick question like: "Does the Bible say 'There is no God'?" Yes, the Bible says that, but it doesn't teach that. What the Bible does teach is that the fool has said it. So we can make the same distinction in bringing out what the Bible reports and what the Bible teaches.

Nevertheless, even though the Old Testament is historically dated, still it was intended for the general and universal profit of all who read it. Look at Hebrews 6:13-20 where it talks about the promise theme, and it says:

> For when God made promise to Abraham, because he could swear by no greater, he sware by himself, saying, surely blessing I will bless thee, and multiplying I will multiply thee. And so, after he had patiently endured, he obtained the promise. For men verily swear by the greater: and an oath for confirmation is to them an end of all strife. Wherein God, willing to show unto the heirs of promise the immutability of his counsel, confirmed it by an oath: That by two immutable things, in which it was impossible for God to lie, [he] might have a strong consolation, who had fled for refuge to lay hold upon the hope set before us.

Does the Bible say "he"? Mine says "we," and that is what the best manuscripts say. *"We* might have a stronger consolation." You and I have "a stronger consolation" because of what God swore to Abraham. *We!* Therefore we can identify. We have strong consolation and hope because of what God did to Abraham. But notice how the text casts the ancient and modern reader as profiting together from a universal word, even though it was given in a definite historical setting.

The same concept is found in the Old Testament, for example, in Hosea 12:3-6. Here Hosea was preaching from Genesis. It is interesting to note that the Old Testament characters preached on the Old Testament. And Hosea said, "He took his brother by the heel in the womb, and by his strength he had power with God." This is a reference to Genesis 25 and 32. It is the Jacob and Esau incident. Hosea continues, "Yea, he had power over the angel, and prevailed: he wept and made supplication unto him: he found him in Bethel, and God spake with. . . ." There God spake with whom? It doesn't say "him." It says, "There God spake with *us.*" "Us" means right down to Hosea's time and audience. We can add also ourselves.

Almost one millennium later, after Jacob's lifetime, it is recorded that when God spoke to Jacob, he spoke not only to Jacob; He spoke also to the "us" of Hosea's time and to the "us" of our time. The R.S.V. translators could not accept that. They put in "him" and then put down the footnote "Hebrew *us.*" They couldn't believe it, but the text in the Hebrew says "us." We weren't there, yet we were addressed in something that appeared time bound.[3]

Perhaps other objections are raised. Someone might say that Christ has put an end to this whole Old Testament teaching. And a text is produced, such as Romans 10:4. Paul concluded a tremendous argument by stating that "Christ is the end of the law." Everybody thinks that he understands what the "end" is. It's the caboose! The end of it is the termination or the cutoff point. But the thing I have the biggest problem with, is that Jesus said in Matthew 5:17 that He had not come "to destroy the law . . . but to fulfill [it]." Now there is a problem. How can we understand this verse? We can understand it by viewing the word "end" as Paul intended it: as the goal of the Law, or the theological conclusion of the Law. Christ is the theological conclusion. This is where the whole thing comes into focus. The Law is leading us to Christ. This is what these writers were trying to say. It was to lead us to Christ. Paul says in Galatians that the Law was the schoolmaster that led us to Christ. In the ancient setting, the Law was like the slave who took the boy to school to be sure that he got there on time. This is what the Law did for us. It took us by the hand and led us to Christ. Christ, then, is the purpose and the goal of the Old Testament.

Even Moses witnessed toward these days. And the gospel that Paul preached is that same word of faith, because he goes on to say in Romans 10:5, "For Moses describeth the righteousness which is of the law." Notice that both verses 5 and 6 are statements made by Moses. One is a quotation from Leviticus 18:5, but Moses also described the righteousness in Deuteronomy 30:10-14. Paul goes on to say the righteousness of faith "speaketh on this wise, say not in thine heart, Who shall ascend into heaven? (that is, to bring Christ down from above:) Or, Who shall descend into the deep? (that is, to bring Christ from the dead.) But what saith

---

3. I am indebted for these points to Patrick Fairbairn, "The Historical Element in God's Revelation" in *Classical Evangelical Essays. . .* , ibid., pp. 67-68.

it?" It what? The word that Moses is describing—what does it say? "The word is nigh thee, even in thy mouth, and in thy heart: that is, the word of faith, which we preach." Paul uses the quotation from Deuteronomy 30:12-14; and he goes on to say that this is the word that he is preaching; it is the same word of faith. It is the same word for both the Old Testament and the New Testament.

But our Lord did put an end, a termination, to the civil and ceremonial aspects of the Law. This also comes out in Hebrews where it says that once for all He appeared to put away the repetition of sacrifices of bulls and goats that could no longer fulfill God's requirements. They had to keep on and on with their sacrificing; and certainly there was an inadequacy there. But Christ has put that away. And by putting that away, the whole focus of God's plans has come to fruition. It all leads to Christ and to His death.

But who can see Christ in the Old Testament, say some, without relying heavily upon the New Testament? Perhaps our Lord never expected anyone to catch on. Maybe these were the deeper things of God. Nevertheless, the truth was there, and Jesus was scolding His contemporaries for being so dull as to miss it. Listen to our Lord make such an indictment on the road to Emmaus, in Luke 24:25–27: "Then he said unto them, O fools, and slow of heart to believe all that the prophets have spoken: Ought not Christ to have suffered these things, and to enter into his glory? And beginning at Moses and all the prophets he expounded unto them in all the scriptures the things concerning himself."

What He said was: "Don't you know your own book, your own history? You should have known beginning with Moses through the testimony of the prophets." And so He began to describe all things concerning Himself. It would have been wonderful to hear that discourse. If we have not seen the central theme of the Old Testament, indeed, all the things concerning Jesus, then we are also "fools and slow of heart" to believe the Old Testament. He says the same thing in Luke 24:44-45. In John 1:45 there was one who was an example of the reverse type, however. Philip found Nathaniel even before any of these events came off. Philip ran up to Nathaniel and said, "We have found him, of whom Moses in the law, and the prophets, did write, Jesus of Nazareth, the son of Joseph."

There is also the story of Anna the prophetess. With Simeon, she recorded her acceptance of this Old Testament truth. At the birth of our Lord, Simeon took the baby in his arms—a little baby —and looking at Him, he said, "Here is the consolation of Israel for which I have been living and waiting. Here is God." But it was only a little baby. Simeon understood from the Old Testament that God was going to send Him in the flesh into our kind of world. These were men and women who believed. They read their Scripture texts well. I wish we had men like that today. Men who would read the whole Word of God (Luke 4:25-38).

I am not against the New Testament. We ought to claim all the New Testament, then say, "But there is more of the Bible; there are thirty-nine books more, all filled with the revelation of God."

In Luke 18:31, Jesus said, ". . . we go up to Jerusalem, and all things that are written by the prophets concerning the Son of man shall be accomplished." Can you imagine the disciples saying to one another, "What is that all about? We don't know anything written about the Son of man that is going to be accomplished in Jerusalem." But our Lord knew what was written. And they were just as obligated to have known about those impending events as we are obligated to know both those that refer to the first coming of Christ, and the ones in the Old Testament that speak of the second coming of Christ with all its grand, accompanying events.

There is a final problem here. Some say that even the prophets themselves and other writers of the Old Testament did not know what they were writing prophetically. But in I Peter 1:9-12, we read that they did know. It is affirmed in Scripture that the prophets did understand what they wrote. So why make an issue? Many do because they question Biblical authority. It is a big question today. Are we reading the text from God's point of view, or are we reading in our own personal ideas? If we are accepting God's authority, that's good. Then we should read and listen carefully.

Finally, why should we bother with the Old Testament? What would we lose if those books were consigned to a corner of history and we became *sola* New Testament students? Isn't it all amplified in the New Testament? The answer is, "No." We would lose much. The doctrine of creation in Genesis 1 and 2, for instance, would be lost. Also the doctrine of the image of God in man would be forgotten. How desperately modern man needs that. He has forgotten that he is being destroyed from the inside out. Another lost doctrine would be the record of how the fall of man took place in our world. A universal plan of salvation is functioning for all men since Eden. (In Romans 16:20, where it says, "And the God of peace shall bruise Satan under your feet shortly," Paul is referring to Genesis 3:15.) In Exodus 20, there is a an absolute standard for a relativistic age. Indeed, God meets man where he is and as he is, even before the Incarnation. God said in Genesis and Exodus that "I shall be your God and you shall be My people, and I shall dwell in the midst of you" (cf. Exod. 29:45-46). What a beautiful text. This theme never dies, not even in New Testament times or our own. Space fails us to tell of the many additional doctrines that are unique to the Old Testament as well as supportive of the New. But our conclusion is certain: we would be poorer without the Old Testament. It would be like having a roof without walls or foundations.

Many people cannot understand what their Lord did for them on the cross. Modern man cannot understand. But it is here in the Old Testament that they can begin to see it. It is a simple picture story with big print. Read it in Leviticus 16. There God made provision for the expiation of sins. It was by the shedding of blood that the guilt of sins was forgiven and removed as far as the east is from the west. Here is an evangelistic message antedating the Christian era.

Scan in your mind's eye such magnificent concepts in our theological history as David's great promise in II Samuel 7, or the doctrine of the incomparable God in Isaiah 40. We find none more beautiful in the whole of Scripture. Nor is there a more superb statement on the Atonement than the theological expression given to it in Isaiah 53. It is still the greatest theological statement of what our Lord did on the cross. And we have an unsurpassed statement on the new heaven and the new earth. Even the Book of Revelation does not surpass the chapters of Isaiah 65 and 66, but simply quotes them. We can read of the future manifestations of the kingdom of God in Daniel 2, 7, and 9. This is an all-too-brief list of the tremendous spiritual assets that we have in the Old Testament. Rather than neglecting the Old Testament, let us turn to it with a new enthusiasm to hear the Word of God and to obey it.

# 2

## The Promise Doctrine

# The Theme of the Old Testament

The Bible is not something that always has to be presented with solemnity and sobriety. There is a happy note within Scripture, and if we can communicate even part of the joy, or—more than that— be happy while we are learning, that will be 75 percent of the educational process. There is joy and laughter in knowing God in Christ, especially as we realize all that He has promised us. Therein lies the subject of this chapter: "The Promise Doctrine."

We have already discussed the problems of sheer apathy and of Biblical ignorance. Another major problem is "spiritualizing" the Bible text. This, in no way, is to be confused with the idea that we must make a Biblical text practical. It is part of our Biblical heritage and wealth that the text of Scripture must communicate to us here and now. Notice, for instance, a passage such as Hebrews 6:18, which leads us to the point where we see that the Bible itself commends this practice. The writer of Hebrews says that the words of Genesis 12 and 22 were given so that ". . . we might have a strong consolation. . . ."

So I am not against the application of a text. I think the text must be applied. This is the only correct conclusion we can reach. Good teaching and good homiletics demand that the conclusion ought to be the high point of sermons and lectures. The last fifty years of teaching and preaching experience in the Americas, however, and perhaps even on the European continent, have been ones in which ministers have specialized in the introduction. They introduce the topic for about ten or fifteen minutes. And since in good Western situations we usually allow only twenty to thirty minutes of total speaking time, little time remains for effective application.

Personally I think we ought to concentrate on the conclusion. It is the high point to which we should bring our listeners. Read some of the great published sermons of the men of a century ago. As they came to the conclusion, they spent two or three pages in the written form. These are high points. As you read you are swept along. You feel the pulse, and even though it is in cold type, you can still sense the live presentation.

I believe this is where we should give more thought and work to our sermons for our time. Application is important. It is to be stressed, and it is a job to which we must give more attention if we are to communicate to our day and age.

Also, I am worried about something else—seriously worried. I'm worried about what we might call an intramural debate. It is something that occurs inside the walls of evangelicalism. We're not fighting any liberals, imagined or real, in this instance. We are talking about Bible-believing evangelicals. Here is the point of my concern: how many interpretations can a Scripture text have?

Many people insist on one interpretation—that is unless you're dealing with prophecy or with typology; or with a text that's rather difficult and you want to say something in spite of what it may have said or despite a lack of understanding of what is said. For many people, the important thing is to "get the blessing," and because "it's still the Word of God, it is able to speak to me." It is here that a serious confusion between *illumination* and *revelation* is made. These two doctrines have been used so interchangeably that I am afraid of what may happen ten years from now in evangelical circles on the problem of *authority*.

Look at the text. Did God say it? Did He speak? Did He speak without stuttering? Is that what the text really means?

I well remember a chapel service in a Christian college that illustrates this issue. We had a wonderful speaker that day, and he had given one of those excellent messages that I've since learned to call "an excellent message, but a poor text." The excellent message went something like this (it was from the Old Testament, and since that's a rarity in itself, why should I complain?): "A widow of one of the sons of the prophets facing foreclosure by her creditors, complained to Elisha. When the prophet learned that all she owned was a little oil, he told her to go and gather in all the containers that she could, take the little bit of oil that was left and to keep pouring it into all of these various vessels. The oil did not stop until the last vessel was filled."

That's the account from II Kings 4:1-6. And it is a good story. But what does it mean? "Do you know," the speaker went on to say, "that in the Bible oil is *always* [and watch that word]—is always—a type of the Holy Spirit." The speaker pressed the point, often made, that as long as we are empty of self and the flesh—as long as we present ourselves as nothing before God—the filling of the Spirit of God will not stop until the last empty Christian is filled.

There were many good things in that chapel message. I can't say all of it was true because it did have a non-Biblical view of personality. I just wonder about the text that was used. The speaker was intent on holding his finger on the text, not on what the text was really saying. Someone later said to me: "It's true, because I got a blessing from it." Well, good for the blessing but bad for the text! It doesn't prove that he received the blessing from that text. It just proves he received a blessing, and that his mind was fertile, able to pull "good" things from various parts of the sermon. How often we "wool gather" from various parts of the Bible, bringing a favorite text back to memory while reading a difficult text. But we must not confuse that "blessing" with what the Spirit is trying to say through that particular verse. Actually we are still thinking of a New Testament passage, or some other passage where that particular doctrine was taught, and then we almost automatically link them all up.

I remember a fellow student going out of that same chapel, and saying, "M-m-m, he didn't preach anything about the woman *selling* the Holy Spirit, as the prophet told her to do in the next verse!" I thought that he was very astute and that he had a legitimate criticism, because as you know, the text does go on to say that she went out and sold the oil. Do we "sell" the Holy Spirit? God forbid! But see what holding a finger on a text or on an interpretation can do?

My last detail would be very hard to apply to that particular message. But it brings up the point that I want to stress, that of the *authority of the Word of God*. We believe that the Bible *is* the Word of God. Of course it is. It is, undoubtedly, God's Word. It is His exact point of view, His estimates, His values, His verbal intention that He is trying to get across through that passage. I believe God speaks not only in His person and in the events of history, but He also speaks in words. He is able to communicate His message, give His value judgments through His men, and so they give a divine point of view. But, mind you, I know nothing about the divine point of view except through the grammar and the written words of these men. They were the chosen men. Revelation came to them.

The Gospels receive a lot of treatment like this. I've heard some wonderful messages, but again I must doubt the text that was used as the basis for each of these messages. Take, for example, the account of the disciples out in the boat of the Sea of Galilee. A great storm came up. Let me quote freely, with imagination, from a "typical" sermon: "We are beset by a number of storms today. There is materialism, there is communism, there are the great issues of ecumenism. They are all swarming in on us. The boat is the Church, and here we are, beset by all of these tremendous forces." Are we? We are not—at least not in that text. But the sermon tells us that there she is, the little Church (I feel so badly about it), about to go under. I've got my finger on the verse. I'm looking at it closely, but I can't see that this was the authoritative point of the writer. What if the twelve disciples were sitting in the front row of a church while I was preaching a message like that; what would they say to each other? Would they whisper, "Did you know that?" Would they shake their heads in amazement? Then we come to the conclusion of our message on the storms. It is a really stirring one, but the conclusion is not the text either!

It's a good message, and I don't want to belittle the message. But the question is the text, which evidently says in the words of our not so mythical preacher: "Have you put your oar in yet? Let's all pull with the Church and get her over to the other side" (of Jordan?). I think that's a Biblical message. We've got to move men and women. We need men who will pull with the Church. We need men who will sense that God is living and doing something in our times. But on the other hand, can I say it with that particular text?

You might say, "What else am I going to do with it? It's just there, it won't say anything else, and I've got to make it say something!" But if you make it say something, then why complain if liberal preachers contend that this is what they've been doing all along? They say that the Bible can *become* the Word of God to you in that moment, and it does; every Sunday morning in many of our pulpits. No! We evangelicals affirm that it *is* the Word of God—written! We believe that, and we sign statements stating that this is so. But I also contend that sometimes our practice belies that theory.

Let us look at the words of the Biblical text. And remember words are important. They are means of communication. Suppose you are in dialogue with someone else, and he says, "Oh I understand what you mean." You come back and you say, "No, I didn't mean that at all. By my use of that word I meant this, and I can show you. See how it was used in my sentence? I only said *this,* so that rules out your meaning altogether. You misunderstood me."

We are sovereign in defining the interpretation of our own words. We have the right to put on any word our distinctive, but legitimate, meaning. For instance, if I should use the word "pen" in a sentence, and you immediately thought it was some sort of little thing you dip into ink, I would say, "No, I meant a ball-point pen." See how I used the word in that sentence and paragraph? I must have the right to let my words carry my own meanings. It is what I say, not what you think I say, that gives it its importance. So must the Biblical authors have the same right!

Let me further illustrate my meaning by the text I Peter 1:9-12. This passage is one of the great texts that everyone runs to as soon as I announce the proposition that there is only one single authoritative meaning for each text. Every text in Scripture has only *one* meaning, but *many* applications. But once we state that there is only one principal singular meaning that is taught in each text, even though it has a wide variety of applications, in different situations of life, people seem to get confused.

Let us set the matter of applications to one side for the moment. Rather, let us go back to *meaning*—the truthfulness and the authority of that text—since this is the real issue of our times.

Some people will say: "But see what Peter says. He is dealing with prophecy when he says, 'surely there were topics on which the prophets wrote, and whose meanings totally or partially eluded them.' " (The slogan in evangelical circles, which some of my colleagues like to use, is that "the prophets wrote better than they knew." I've heard that so often, and I was even taught it in my own formative years and in school. Now I wonder if that was so.)

Look at the text, I Peter 1:9–12: "Receiving the end of your faith [that's the same word used in Romans 10:4, the *telos.* It's the teleological end, or the *goal,* of our faith], even the salvation of your souls, of which salvation the prophets have inquired and searched diligently. . . ." Did the prophets scratch their heads? Yes, they did. The text says so. ". . . who [the antecedent goes back to "prophets"] prophesied of the grace that should come unto you." The prophets were talking about the good news, the grace of God, the righteousness that should come to us, "Searching [as in the idea of searching in verse 10] what or what manner of time the Spirit of Christ which was in them did signify. . . ."

"Searching what, or what manner of time." Now if you go through the various translations, a good majority of them read this way: "Searching what *person* or what time." The italicized word does not appear in the Greek text. There are two words that are connected here: "what," and "what manner of time." Both of them, as you will discover from most Greek grammars, form a tautological statement. That is, they are saying over again the same thing, repeating the same idea, both modifying the one word "time."[1]

The point Peter was making here is that what the prophets did not know is the *time,* the very same thing you and I don't know, with regard to the second coming of our Lord. But I think we know much, apart from the time. We have no idea whether it is to be mid-morning, mid-afternoon, or any other part of the day. And we have no idea as to what month or year it will be. But I do know that we should be ready. I do know that my Lord may come soon and we should be watching for Him. So the text here says that what the prophets did not know—what they were searching for (incidentally the same thing Daniel searched for at the end of the Book of Daniel) was the *time.* And as Daniel, and Zechariah also, asked the *time* question (and there are a lot of questions in their books), the interpreting angel who appeared to both of these prophets, said, "Don't you understand what you read?" And when they did not understand, they were helped.

So the angel said: "This is what it means." Perhaps that's why Daniel, for at least his first nine chapters, is easily understood; he said, "I don't undersand." Then the Spirit of God gave to Daniel, and thus to us, the interpretation.

We find the same thing in the Book of Zechariah. Perhaps if we had been there, we would have put up our hand, and asked the

---

1. I have already argued this case in some detail in my article, "The Eschatological Hermeneutics of 'Evangelicalism': Promise Theology," *Journal of the Evangelical Theological Society* 13 (1970):91-99, especially pp. 94-96.

angel even more questions like: "What's this? What's that?" Fortunately (or unfortunately, depending upon your point of view) there still is some work left, and some room for us to do some work.

Nonetheless the verses of I Peter 1:9-12 are very, very plain. What the prophets did not know was the *time;* nor did they know the manner or the special circumstances of that time. But what they did know is significant. For the text goes on to say, ". . . when it testified beforehand the sufferings of Christ, and the glory that should follow. Unto whom it was revealed, that not unto themselves, but unto us, did they minister. . . ."

There are at least five things here, depending on how you count them.

*First,* they knew that they were speaking about the Messiah—about Christ—when they testified beforehand concerning the sufferings of Christ. Now some make of the idea of searching that they were searching concerning this also. No! They were searching concerning only the *time;* time was the object of searching. It wasn't that they were searching concerning Christ. They were searching concerning the time that was signified when they spoke beforehand about Christ.

*Second,* they knew that they were talking about the sufferings of Christ.

*Third,* they knew that they were talking about the glory that would be His.

*Fourth,* they knew the order, because it was the glory that should follow; it was sufferings first, glory last. Our Lord wasn't going to be glorified and then suffer. He was to suffer and then be glorified. They knew this to be the order.

And *fifth,* they knew that it was revealed to them that they were not ministering only to themselves, but as verse 12 says: ". . . unto us did they minister the things which are now reported unto you. . . ."

What a beautiful demonstration this is. I am as confident as I can be—as confident as grammar can make it—that this text is very, very plain. The point is, that what they did not know was the *time,* but what they *did know* was that they were ministering concerning the Messiah, the Christ. They did know that they were ministering concerning His sufferings and concerning His glory.

They knew the order. And they knew finally that they were also ministering to us.

Now if all this is true, and if the prophets themselves knew what they were saying, then what really was their theme? How did it lead into the New Testament times? How could they have had the same Lord, the same gospel, and the same hope that we share today?

Perhaps we can go back and begin by tracing the main theme of the Old Testament. If we only had the ability to keep a proper focus as we go through the Old Testament, perhaps we wouldn't be so distracted or so disconcerted with the number of things that we aren't able to handle initially. If only we knew what the central theme was throughout the thirty-nine books, what deeper understanding would be ours.

I would like to suggest that the main theme of the Old Testament is "the promise." How do I dare say that it is the promise? Because some forty times in the New Testament this word *epaggelia* (almost like the word *euaggelia,* or the gospel, the good news, which is a word that is related to it) is mentioned. And almost fifty times there is a reference to it in the majority of the New Testament books as they reflect upon the Old Testament. And these references indicate that this promise is a single promise, that it has a continuity as it develops, and many specifications are added through the history of revelation as we come into the New Testament period.[2]

There is a consistent hermeneutic here. You have a unified people with a unified purpose who have their eyes single toward this promise. Since the word "promise" is repeated so often in the New Testament's appeal to the Old Testament, we urge Christians to follow this authoritative lead and use it as an organizing category for integrating the messages of the Old and New Testaments.

But where does it begin? I suggest that it begins in Genesis 3:15, which was known at the time it was given to be a Messianic prediction. That is, it falls into a long line of Messianic passages. Now it's true, as we read the text and as we look at Genesis 3:15, that sometimes it doesn't seem possible that the original writer intended

---

2. One of the finest books ever to explore this topic is still available. Willis J. Beecher, *The Prophets and the Promise* (Grand Rapids: Baker Book House, 1963), reprint of the 1905 edition.

all of that meaning in those few words. Sometimes it looks as if we're reading something into it—a direct violation of all our preceding argument on the single meaning of the text.

But what about the previous comment in regard to the single meaning of the text? I would still affirm that the single meaning of this text is that there is a surprise "Person" who is coming as the antidote for the whole mess that Adam and Eve have gotten themselves and their posterity into as a result of the Fall.

Genesis 3:15 tells us of the curse on the serpent, which was announced in verse 14. In verse 15, God goes on to say, "And I will put enmity [enmity, I remind you, is a word that is not used between animals or between men and animals, but is always used between persons. It is a very specialized word in the vocabulary, if you take Old Testament usage into account], . . . I will put enmity between thee and the woman, and between thy seed and her seed."

The King James Version really slipped here. It says *"It* shall bruise thy head, and thou shalt bruise his heel." Now what is being talked about here? Is this the place where girls really first became afraid of snakes? Is this why most girls stand on chairs, if there is one handy, when they see a snake, and scream for some deliverer to come? Is it just some innate, psychological fear of the serpent?

The text altogether excludes that when it says "I will put enmity." Notice that the enmity is divinely implanted. This has nothing to do with the psychology of the person. The text says that God implanted this enmity between the two of them, and it says that it is to be between "thee" (the woman) and Satan. Of that there is no question.

The serpent is always *the serpent.* From the very beginning of time, there has been a world in which the supernatural was much more real than it seems to be to us today. The one who is mentioned here is no less than Satan himself.

Genesis 3:1 says, "The serpent was more subtle than any beast of the field. . . ." Do you see how the King James translators said it in Genesis 3:1? In Hebrew, the same expression found in Genesis 3:1 is found also in Genesis 3:14. But this time there apparently was a split in the translation committee, and so they must have decided on a compromise in order to get home. In Genesis 3:1 they said, *"than* any beast of the field." That would be a partitive sense, and would put "the serpent" in the biological class of serpents. But in Genesis 3:14 it says, "thou are cursed *above* all cattle." It's the same Hebrew phrase. I would like to suggest to you that both renderings should be "above" and that it should be a comparative use in both senses.

The Hebrew means literally "from all." By the time the translators got to Genesis 3:14, it was quite obvious that the reference here was not to the "little creepers" that had been called "good" by God. Perhaps we have forgotten that in chapter 1 of Genesis it is recorded that God made crawlers, looked at them, and declared them "good." Because things slither along the ground it doesn't mean that they have had the curse placed on them. God designed some animals to have their locomotion in that manner.

When it says "upon thy belly shalt thou go, and dust shalt thou eat all the days of thy life," we note that very same phrase occurs six times in the Old Testament. Checking these contexts, I think the fact will be borne out that the expression is metaphorical. It is metaphorical because reptiles do not actually "eat" dust or dirt. They may inhale some, but it is not part of their diet. It indicates, rather, a place of submission. Here is a promise that "the serpent" (Satan himself) is to be cursed *above* all the cattle, yea *above* every beast of the field; and his position of humility is assured, for upon his belly shall he go, face down, prostrate before the King of kings. The text says, "I will put enmity between thee [Satan] and the woman."

Mark this with numbers as Leupold does in his Genesis commentary.[3] Make Satan number 1 and the woman number 2. The contest is to be 1 versus 2. And then, "between thy seed" (make Satan's seed 3) versus her seed (make the woman's seed number 4). So we have 1 versus 2 and 3 versus 4. Now here comes the surprise. "He shall bruise thy head." Where did *"He"* come from? The text contains a third-person, masculine, singular independent pronoun—*"He."* The Douay Version renders it "she." I don't know where they got that rendering, but I know why they wanted it there. But the text says *"He"* whereas the King James Version says *"it."* There is no word for "it" unless the third-person, masculine, singular pronoun is here functioning, as it often

3. H. C. Leupold, *Exposition of Genesis,* vol. 1 (Grand Rapids: Baker Book House, 1953), pp. 163-70.

does, for the neuter. The context leads us to expect some person who will belong to the seed of the woman. At any rate, "He shall bruise thy head and thou [referring back to number 1] shalt bruise his heel." Look at this: We have 1 versus 2 and 3 versus 4. Then, surprise of surprises, 4a, a masculine descendant of the woman's seed, will oppose none other than "the serpent," or 4a versus 1. That's what the text says.

Perhaps you say, that's not a whole lot of Messianic teaching. In a way I agree. But it does tell you the outcome of history. We've gotten into tremendous trouble with the Fall. All Christian theology is in response to what took place in the Fall. We are against evil, we hate evil. We've built a whole theology in relationship to the problem of evil, especially personal evil. This is what salvation is all about; it's the saving of men's lives in personal redemption.

But there is more to it than that. Romans 8 says that we will also see the redemption of the whole ecological problem. This is what most everyone is concerned about. Nature itself is out of order because of what has happened to man. Nature is groaning, as a woman in travail, waiting for the redemption that is to be found in Christ Jesus our Lord, so that the whole of the cosmos—man first and then the whole of nature itself—is to be wrapped up, redeemed, cleansed, and brought back to its Creator. Can it be done? It will be done.

How do we know? The text says so. Who will do it? One of this first woman's descendants. Someone from her seed (and the word "seed" is collective, a corporate identity or a whole group, which can be so narrowed as to focus in upon one individual) is going to do this great work. That individual is not announced here, but we know who He is. He has already appeared. He is Christ.

But the word "seed" (and Paul rightfully makes a big play on this word in Galatians 3:16) is not plural, even though he knows the difference between a collective and a plural noun. He knows that it isn't "seeds." It would be like trying to say "deers" in English. You have a deer and deer. There is one, and there are many. This is a phenomenon evident in most languages. So what is Paul's big point? His big point is that out of the collective body of this woman's descendants, the "Israel of God," there is a narrowing down to one who shall preeminently represent the whole group. This is Christ Jesus Himself.

But at this point the text had said it is 4a versus 1—the Christ to

be born versus Satan. But you may say, "Are you sure that anyone ever had this idea before the Christian century?" Yes. There is
an article that appeared in the 1965 issue of the *Journal of Biblical
Literature* (which is not exactly an evangelical organ in the Americas, representing, as it does, mainly liberal scholarship), and it was
written by Ralph Martin. It deals with the earliest pre-Christian
interpretation of Genesis 3:15, which could be demonstrated. He
took the Septuagint rendering of this text (the Septuagint comes
from the third century B.C.) and demonstrated beyond a shadow
of a doubt, on philological grounds, that the Jewish community—
at least the one in Alexandria—understood this to be Messianic,
and this well in advance of the birth of Christ. This came not by
spiritualizing or allegorizing the text, but by a similar method to
that which we have just discussed above, emphasizing this third
masculine pronoun.

For the next greatest moment in the history of revelation, we
turn to Genesis 12:3, where we have a further spelling out of
this "promise." It began with a command. The Lord gave a command to Abraham that he was to leave the Babylonian country, his
kindred, and his father's house, to journey into a land that He
would show him. The content of that ancient word in Genesis 3:15
is now enlarged. Not only will man's Deliverer ultimately vanquish
Satan, but God has selected the man Abraham and has given to
him the promise of a seed—a land, a nation, a great name—and
that all the nations of the earth shall be blessed through this man
and his descendants, especially that "He" who is to come in this
seed.

I don't think that this last item is to distract us, because five
times this aspect of the promise is specifically repeated in Genesis,
and it always occurs in a final or climactic position. Further, we
insist, on good grammatical grounds, that this verb should always
be translated as a passive, "be blessed," and not as some modern
versions say, "bless themselves." This holds true up to the time of
Joseph and on into the Book of Exodus. It would be interesting
to study how many times from chapter 12 of Genesis through
chapter 50, this promise doctrine and theme occurs in implicit and
explicit statements. Perhaps forty to fifty times, over and over
again, this becomes the great hope of the people. It is the hope not
only of Abraham to whom God promised a "seed"—still repeating what has been given to Eve in Genesis 3:15—but, now is also

the hope of a "people." And God adds the ultimate in blessing: "I will be your God." This becomes a theological phrase that rings from the patriarchal narrative in Genesis 12 on into the New Testament Book of Revelation. And more than that: through this seed everybody else is to receive a blessing. Here is the missionary mandate, that the gospel is open to all men. The announcement of this one Man and His work is the message, the good news that all men can be released, or "saved," from the effects of the Fall.

That is my understanding of this passage. It is also Paul's understanding, as we see in Galatians 3:6-8. There he calls it the gospel which was beforehand preached to Abraham. And it is the same word of faith, he says in Romans, which is now being preached to us.

Continuing through the Book of Genesis and on into the Book of Exodus, a second proposition is added to this theme: "I will be your God." It is a beautiful promise in itself. The God who is so far off, who is transcendent (or as they said during the Barthian era—"God is the totally other One"—in direct opposition to the extremes of the liberal era, when God was so "buddy, buddy" and everyone's Father and Brother). God is transcendent; He is holy; He is altogether different from us sinful men. Ontologically, in His being, He is different. Morally, He is different. We are sinners— He is holy. As a corrective to Karl Barth's definition of God as "totally other . . . ," in this text God volunteers to be a personal God to the patriarchs and their children.

That is beautiful, but it's only the half of it. The patriarchal narrative includes God saying, "I will be your personal God." But in the Book of Exodus something is added to it: "and you shall be My people." In Exodus 19 particularly, He says: "You shall be My peculiar possession." Note the word "peculiar." Be careful how you use the King James Version here, for to us the word "peculiar" means a fellow with idiosyncrasies, someone who's not altogether with it. But in Hebrew, the word is a *segullah,* "a movable possession." It's a treasure that a person can take up and carry off with him. It is opposite to real property, such as real estate, which refers to unmovable land. God says, "I will be a God to you and you shall be My people, My "movable treasure." Then adding to that, in the latter part of the Book of Exodus (29:45-46), He announces in connection with the tabernacle, "And I will dwell ['tabernacle,' or 'pup-tent']" with you. Thus God also will personally make His abode with His people of promise.

God, who in His shekinah glory comes, will also *shakan,* i.e., dwell, tabernacle or "pup-tent" with His people. That's precisely where John chapter 1 begins: "The Word [Jesus] was made flesh and dwelt [pup-tented] among us." Do you understand that the high and holy God has come and invaded our planet? He has become part of our history. We're the visited planet. God Himself has come here. He was here! He is here! He moved into our history, into our geography. Were we to think of a Christianity in which there would be no Christmas or Easter, it would be all over. Christianity would be finished. Life itself would be finished as far as meaning and purpose are concerned.

If a man wants to challenge my Christian faith, he can claw at God's sovereignty or he can go after a lot of other doctrinal subtleties, such as the Trinity, that give him problems. But if someone really wants to destroy Christianity, let him tear down the Resurrection. Remember, when you go through real periods of doubt (certainly Satan is not beyond putting many of you through this) that the central part of your Christian faith still stands on the One who came back from the dead! Paul said it in I Corinthians 15 over and over again. Read that chapter as the stronghold, the central part, of your faith.

God said: "I will be your God—you shall be My people, and I will come into the midst, and I will dwell with you." How does this tie in with our study of the promise doctrine?

It is still the promise that there will be victory over Satan. Christ (the Seed) shall succeed. Here again is the promise through the seed of woman. Would God do that through human seed, really? Why would He do that? Why humanize it? Why come down where we live? But God accomplished this down here where we live. Can you understand God's accommodation to men, so that we might know? There can be no excuse. God has done everything. Only believe! Only receive!

The date on your calendar is A.D., "the year of our Lord." What is so important about it? By this we are thrown back constantly to the main focus of history, I think deliberately, by the providence of God.

Not only is it through Eve's seed and Abraham's seed, but this promise continues to develop in the Book of Exodus and throughout the rest of the Old Testament. Finally it is fulfilled in the New Testament: "The Word was made flesh." "Immanuel, God with us." This transcendent God also is the God who came down to dwell with us.

Let us return to John chapter 1, for just one other observation. I was surprised recently to notice that John in certain aspects of this chapter is referring back to the argument in Exodus. He says in John 1:17: "For the law was given by Moses, *but* grace and truth came by Jesus Christ." We're going to deal with that "but" later. In the KJV, the word "but" is italicized, which does not mean for emphasis. (I heard of a fellow who preached on all of the italicized words in the Bible, believing those words were the ones the Holy Spirit wanted emphasized!) Those are not the words that the Spirit chose as most important. Those are the words that the translators added only to smooth out the English reading of the text.

But now for the main point. John goes on to say that "no man hath seen God at any time; the only begotten Son, which is in the bosom of the Father, he hath declared him." He has just said in verse 15: "John bare witness of him, and cried, saying, This was he of whom I spake, He that cometh after me is preferred before me: for he was before me."

Now look at the phrase "is preferred before me," or "ranks before me." In Greek that word is translated in every other context in a temporal sense. I can't find one instance in all of the Greek language, not one instance in the New Testament or in any of the papyri, in which it is to be translated as a "ranking ahead of me." In all the cases that I'm aware of, it means "before me." It occurs some thirty times in the New Testament Greek, and it is used quite extensively outside the New Testament.

What then is he saying? "He that cometh after me was before me, for He *was* before me." You say, that's tautological; he's saying the same thing that occurs later on. But he is not. You must see the difference in the Greek verb that occurs with the use of both "befores." He says that the one who comes after me *was here historically* before me, for He *existed* before me. John uses the verb "to be" in that second instance.

I found this interpretation in Frederick Godet's commentary on John. Godet was the noted Free Churchman of the middle of the last century. But I also saw it in E. W. Hengstenberg's commentary on John. Here were two Old Testament commentators digging into the New Testament, and I thought this to be amazing. Godet quoted—in this Johannine context—references from the Book of Exodus. If that point of view is sustained, then John said: "Here comes one who is coming after me, but let me tell you something, He's already been here, historically, for He was here from eternity." What a beautiful verse. This speaks of the eternality of the Son, and also speaks of the fact that He was here historically, even before his historic "in-fleshment" at that first Christmas.

Let me quickly trace the scenes for you with a quick sweep through the rest of the Old Testament. In moving into the rest of the Pentateuch you will see that the key chapter is II Samuel 7, where David is now promised to be the one through whose family the promise is going to come. But David is told that he is not to build his projected temple for the Lord. David before had said to Nathan, "Nathan, I think I'm going to build a house for the Lord." Nathan responded, "The Lord bless you, do everything that's in your heart" (cf. II Sam. 7:1-3).

That night the Lord spoke to Nathan, and said, "Not so." (This is rather interesting, for not everything that a prophet says is inspired. Only when a prophet in the Bible says, "Thus saith the Lord," and announces it as a conscious revelation from God, is it inspired.) "This is what you shall tell David. Don't give him your opinion, but rather give him this message from the Lord. The message from the Lord is that I will make a house out of you. You don't need to build me a house. Your son, as a matter of fact, will build the house after I have secured and established your dynasty without your own kingdom-building efforts."

Then, in the middle of that chapter, God through Nathan announces an amazing thing. He says to David, "I will be a father to your son [another collective term like "seed"] and he will be a son to Me." This will be perpetual. This will be for all generations, and this is to be the "law of humanity." King David was staggered by the sweeping implications of what he has just received. He felt completely unworthy of the huge honor conferred on him. Almost all modern versions have missed the meaning of II Samuel 7:19b. They hear David say something like "manner" or "custom," but this can never translate a Hebrew word like *Torah,* which means "law" or "instruction." So does I Chronicles 17:17b, where it repeats the same comment of David, "And Thou art regarding me according to the uplifting instruction for humanity, O Lord God!" What is this "charter of humanity"? What is this law of humanity? The charter for all mankind is that David's Son is to be the one who is to carry the promise, and through David's Son will come the blessing that was promised to the whole earth, as far back as the time of Eve, Abraham, and Moses.[4]

This is where the prophets pick up the theme and carry it on. Read Isaiah 7:7 through chapter 9, Isaiah chapter 53, and many others. The psalmist picks it up, too. Read Psalm 89, where there is a commentary on II Samuel 7, glorifying God for what He's done in the Davidic dynasty. Read Psalm 2, Psalm 110, Psalm 22, and Psalm 72. All of these speak of the centrality of this "Man of Promise," who is coming, just as men were led to believe by the promise doctrine. He will be called the Son of man, and He will become the Sin-bearer for all mankind.

This is the message of promise, and it's found in Genesis 12:3, as well as in Leviticus 16: the Man of Promise and the work of the promise.

In Leviticus 16, where the day of atonement is described, we have a beautiful revelation of God Himself. If you have never understood Christian justification or what happens in the reconciliation process, you ought to be able to see it in this big "picture-book story form" in Leviticus 16. It's so plain. I don't see how anybody could miss what our Sin-bearer has done. The two goats that are brought in for one sin-offering show this so clearly.

Move into the Historical Books and read II Samuel 7 and its parallel passage in I Chronicles 17. From the Books of the Prophets, read the Isaiah 7–9 passage and its parallel on the Atonement in Isaiah 52:13 through the rest of Isaiah 53. What pictures these are of the Atonement in fulfillment of the promise!

Where shall we look for the promise in the Wisdom Books? Probably the central chapters would be Psalm 89 and 110. These are the chapters which, if understood, can be stepping stones that will help carry us through the whole of the Old Testament.

How am I so assured this is so? Look and see what the New Testament says when it comes to rehearse the message of the

---

4. See my forthcoming article, "The Blessing of David: The Charter for Humanity," in *The Law and the Prophets: a Festschrift to Oswald T. Allis* (Nutley, N.J.: Presbyterian and Reformed Publishing Co., 1973).

Old Testament. Stephen, being judged, refers to the promise that was given to the fathers, and then he begins explicating this theme (cf. Acts 6, 7).

See also what is done in the Pauline literature. See what happens in the Book of Hebrews and what occurs in the General Epistles. Everywhere we see the promise doctrine, a promise which was not only for those men but also for you and for me.

I am represented in that triumph of God—a triumph that began at Calvary in which our Lord announced the second "It is finished" in the history of this world. He pronounced the first "It is finished" on the sixth day of creation, to mark the cessation of initial creative activity. On the cross He uttered those last words, which I believe are from Psalm 22, "It is finished"—marking the cessation of the provision for our means of atonement, the basis upon which our reconciliation with God is provided. There yet shall come one more "It is finished," which will be the break between history and the ages spent with God. That comes in the Book of Revelation.

What is the dominant theme in all of these Scriptures? It is the *content* of the covenant. It is the promises themselves. I use "promises" in the plural because the one promise of God has many specifications. I wish I could show you that it's not just Messianic. It aims not just at the Messianic person of Christ. It includes the gospel and everything else along with it. And it ties all these doctrines in together very, very beautifully.

The text is there. It's living. Perhaps it's a little dead for some people. Get back and put your eye on the central focus. Meet your Lord, and having met your Lord, then venture out to some of the chapters on either side of it, and pretty soon the whole of the Old Testament will take on for you, not just a preface, not just background material, but a grand symphony with several parts —all of them contributing to the central theme of our Christian life.

# 3

# The Law of the Lord

## Teaching the Paths of Life

This chapter will deal with what is probably the most difficult subject in teaching the Old Testament. This is the topic that, more than any other, causes people to forsake the Old Testament. And they do so, evidently, because of one thing—the Law, or the Law of the Lord, to give it the more complete title.

When most people read the Old Testament, they do so with the feeling that they are familiar with the "promise" made with the patriarchs in Genesis. Then they come to the Book of Exodus where they run into the Law. And as Gerhard Von Rad has summarized in his *Old Testament Theology*[1] (many others have repeated the same assessment of the situation), this is one problem above all others that causes many people to drop the Old Testament and move on into the New. Therefore, as an introduction to this chapter, let us examine the matter of the Law itself.

First of all, consider some of the New Testament passages, since these are more familiar, especially the Pauline words, with regard to the Law. To many readers, Paul often seems to have quite a negative attitude to the Law. And in a quick reading of the New Testament Epistles, it seems as if he says: "We've had it with the Law; it's all over, so let's forget about it."

But I have a real problem here, and I cannot forget it. Nor do I think that that is what Paul said, or even intended. My personal problem is that I am a teacher of the Old Testament. But more than that, I have other problems. For instance, I read what the psalmist said about the "Law of the Lord" in Psalm 19. What is he so excited about? Why does he find the Law such a blessing? How can he say that the "Law of the Lord is perfect, able to convert the soul, able to make wise the simple, more to be desired than

---

1. Gerhard Von Rad, *Old Testament Theology*, vol. 2 (New York: Harper and Row, 1965), p. 390.

honey, yea than gold"? He also assures us that the "Law" is to be desired above everything else.

Then I read Psalm 119, and it seems as if here the writer, in this the longest Psalm, praises God's Law over and over again. (Talk about emptying one's guns! The psalmist just gives it everything he has!) Rather than the Law being a curse, suddenly the Law is seen to be a blessing. Or again, Psalm 1:1 and 2 says, "Blessed is the man . . . [whose] delight is in the law of the Lord. . . ." Yet in the New Testament Paul seems to say "Cursed is the man who listens to that Law." Who is right? Do we have a Biblical contradiction here? Or do we have something that has been phased out? Let us search the Scriptures and see.

In the first place, let us examine the Law's relationship to the ministration of the Holy Spirit. In II Corinthians 3:9-11, there is just such a comparison between the ministry of the Spirit and the ministry of the Law. Here it seems to say that the one is "the ministry of death" whereas the other is "the ministry of life," which is much more glorious. How are we to answer this? May I suggest that the answer lies in what Paul writes in verse 6: "Who also hath made us able ministers of the new testament; not of the letter, but of the spirit: for the letter killeth, but the spirit giveth life."

This particular verse has been quoted so frequently that most people have understood "the letter" to mean the Old Testament. They have read the word here as if the Greek said *graphē,* which they equate with the Old Testament; then they read the "spirit" as if that word refers to the New Testament. But the truth of the matter is that the Greek word here is not *graphē;* it's *gramma,* from which we get "grammar," or at least the root for it. Hence what he is talking about is the "outward form" merely, not the spiritual import nor the content of that Law. And he says that the Law is a "glorious ministration" of condemnation which is "done away with" (the Greek word for "done away with" is *katargeō*), and he uses those words in verse 11. Paul talks about that which is done away with, while a much more glorious ministration of the Spirit and righteousness remains.

But, I would argue here, be careful not to read this section too quickly. The question here is: "Is it the Law or is it the ministry of Moses that is being compared to the ministry of the gospel?" And to even ask that question, I think, is to also give the answer.

What Paul is contrasting is not the content of the Law, but rather the ministry of the one through whom the Law came. And rather than "the letter" equaling the Law in the Old Testament, and "the Spirit" equaling the New Testament, we find here that he is talking about the outward, formal, ostensible parts of both Testaments, versus the internal, living, vitalizing ability of both Testaments which is able to make alive!

I might remind you in this context, that if you really think that the text says that the Old Testament was a ministration of death, then just refer back to II Corinthians 2:15-16, and see that the gospel can become "a savour of death unto death" also. Not because the gospel has death within itself, but rather because of the *shape* and *condition* of man to whom that gospel comes.

That gospel can sometimes come to men and make them alive because they receive it. It's like the seed falling on prepared ground. But for other men, the gospel can come to them, and not having a prepared soil—a prepared heart—the result is just the opposite. Then it becomes a savour of death unto death. Not intrinsically, mind you, but relatively. And again, we must remember it is especially with regard to men, not with regard to the content of the message itself. Someone has said that "the same sun that softens wax, will harden clay." This might serve to illustrate what we are groping after.

The next point to be considered is the Law's relationship to faith. In Romans 3 there is a word used, *katargeō*, which means to make idle, inactive, or abolish. It is the same word as that used in II Corinthians 3:11. Has the Law become passé for us today? Can we not use this old Biblical word? Wouldn't this be a good excuse, if indeed it has been declared to be obsolete, for cutting short part of our Bible study program? We could do away with much of the academic curriculum in Biblical studies, which is too long already! We could say, "Forget the Law, it has been rendered inactive."

The text that should be considered here, however, is Romans 3:31: "Do we then make void the law through faith?" That's the precise question I would like to ask, since it is also the one Paul asked in that passage: "Do we then make void the Law—especially now that faith is here?" Now notice that Paul himself, who wrote the II Corinthians 3:11 passage, here uses the identical Greek verb in Romans 3:31 when he asks, "Do we do away with

51

the Law because faith has come?" Then listen to his answer. And it comes with every negative that we know of, in any language. Basically, the KJV says, "God forbid," which is a sort of free translation of "Never!" "No!" "May it never be true!"

He says that we do not do away with the Law through faith. So I must understand that Paul himself is not anti-Law. He has asked the same question, the very same foolish question I was attempting to ask, and he says, "No, faith has not replaced it." "Rather," he says, "we establish the Law by faith." And from here Paul goes on to talk about other passages in Romans, of "the obedience of faith" (1:15 and again in 16:26).

In the third place, having discussed the Law's relationship to the ministration of the Spirit, and the Law's relationship to faith, what about the Law's relationship to salvation, or justification? Is there any relationship? My own answer is: No, there is none! There is no relationship whatsoever. That is precisely what we ought to brand as legalism. Actually, legalism is not "doing" the Law, nor is legalism "observing" the commandments that God has given. Rather, legalism is that perversion, that abuse, and that malignancy and wasteful use of the Law, which believes that salvation can be obtained by keeping the Law.

To use the Law as a crutch to get into heaven, is to fall into the same trap that Paul condemns in every one of his Epistles. That is legalism. It is the attempt to climb up into heaven "some other way." It is the attempt to make void the grace of God, and especially Christ's death upon the cross. This is the wrong type of redemption center. It is replacing the "giftiness" of God with trading-stamp books, in which we take so many books to God and we ask Him, "Now may I have that package of salvation?"

There are some people who like to think of the Law as a sort of redemption center, to which they take so many merit books and say: "Now, Lord, will You help me on that exam, even though I didn't study? I do have many books of merits here, as You can see." It is a trap we can easily fall into. It is a bypassing of the grace of God, a malignancy attached to the Law itself. This is legalism, which will indeed make void the death of Christ. It's anti-New Testament, anti-Christian, and it's anti-Old Testament. Paul hated it, Moses hated it, and our Lord hates it. It's anti-everything that is good, Godly, and Biblical. It is wrong!

Never—but never—is there a record of anyone ever getting into heaven by works, either in the Old Testament or in the New Testament. Neither was there ever such a hypothetical offer even made.[2] If there had been, we would have put our finger on the verse, and we would have used it. But I cannot find such a text in Scripture at all. In fact, Paul himself says the opposite. In Galatians 3:21b he argues, "If there had been given a law which could have given life, verily righteousness should have been by the law." But alas, there was no such law. So how can we confuse the Law and justification?

Some people think that the rich young ruler is an illustration of the promise of eternal life through keeping the Law. But I remind you that our Lord Himself was handling that case. The rich young ruler came up to Him and said, "What must I do to inherit eternal life?" Or it can be translated, "How can I be saved?" And the Lord said to him, "Keep the commandments." Now why did He say that? Was He trying to say they were still under the old program—that the new program had not begun because Calvary had not yet come? Some think so.

On the other hand, see what Jesus said in that passage. The man replied, "I've kept all the commandments." But he still wasn't saved. It seems that the Lord then built a special case for a special individual. He knew what was wrong with this man. He knew precisely where the roadblock was in his committing himself to the Savior.

So when the man said, "I have kept all these from my youth up," see how our Lord moved in on him. He was a masterful soul-winner. He went immediately to the core problem. Jesus said: "Why don't you give all of your goods to the poor?" The man said, "I can't do that, I'm rich." He had another god, another loyalty, another commitment. Actually he was not even keeping the first commandment of the Law. Can you imagine the surprise of the disciples when they came back later on? They, too, didn't understand grace and the free gift. When they asked, "Lord, who then can be saved?" they showed that they also had it wrong.

There are people today who run after our Lord and say, "Lord,

---

2. For a more detailed discussion of this point, see Walter C. Kaiser, Jr., "Leviticus 18:5 and Paul: 'Do This and You Shall Live (Eternally?)'" *Journal of the Evangelical Theological Society* 14 (1971):19-28, especially p. 20.

You gave him the plan for full commitment. You didn't first give him the basic steps that lead to commitment. You should have given him the plan, the basic plan: No. 1—God loves you and has a wonderful plan for your life," and so on. Or, "You should have started out basically with him, but now You tell him about full surrender. Isn't that too much at first?" Not at all. Our Lord knows that unless He is Lord of all, He is not Lord at all. I often think we've got "Saviorship" and "Lordship" all confused, so that in principle we have not understood that a man cannot give his heart to the Lord, without giving himself.

It is well understood that to love a person with all of one's heart is to love that person with one's whole self. You can't give anything less; you can't give anything more. It's "me." "Heart" really stands for "me." Perhaps it's just a figure of speech, but when we say that we love the Lord our God with all our heart, with all our soul, and that we believe in Him with all our heart, there is a totality in it that leaves nothing out.

As far as I know, I commit all of myself to Him: body, soul, and spirit. And that's what our Lord was pointing out when He took the rich young ruler right to the crux of the matter, to the heart of the issue. That man was willing intellectually and emotionally to come to Christ. But he also said in effect, "I've got a few things here. I've got this little bit of idolatry. You won't mind if I hang on to it, will You, Lord? In everything except my money and possessions, Lord?" No! All that has to come under the judgment and control of the Lord, too. This is not legalism either. It's Biblical faith.

In the fourth place, we ask: what is the Law's relationship to sanctification? There is here a very definite relationship. The promise still continues, even as we discuss the Law. It is not supplanted. There is a basic relationship that we have already established with the Lord; but as we go on with Him, the Law also has everything to do with that relationship to, and fellowship with, the Lord.

In I Timothy 1:8 we read: "The law is good, if a man use it lawfully [rightly]." In that context, and others as well, we must understand the moral aspects of the Law. For instance, in Galatians 2:14 and Colossians 2:16, Paul writes about circumcision, saying that this rite has been done away with. It has been abolished. On the other hand, in I Corinthians 9:21, he wants Christians to be "in-lawed" to Christ. And further, he says in Romans 13:8 and 10 that "love is the fulfilment of the law." He then tells us what he means by the Law, by repeating six of the ten commandments. The same thing is repeated in Galatians 5:14 and 6:2.

Notice that in each case, love does not replace the Law as a new Christian ideal. Joseph Fletcher made that mistake in his situation ethics. For example, Fletcher proposes that everything is all right in an ethical decision between two people if they do it in love. If they decide to have illicit sexual relations together, but they both do it in the context of love, it is all right. He presumes that love has become the content. But love is never the moral content in the decision. Love is only the motive to the fulfillment of the Law. Love itself can never be the content. Love can only be the stimulus, the emotion, or the motivating force, which points me toward that ethical decision that I must make, or that I am being forced to make.

Neither can we say that the Law of Christ is a new Law that releases us from the old and sets up new criteria for living, since the Law of Christ is identified with the content of the previous Law.

But that would not be an easy way out of the situation either. Besides, there is this one great consideration, and I would ask you to remember this even if you don't remember anything else about this discussion. If New Testament people like ourselves are freed from the moral aspects of the Law that God gave in the Old Testament, and then repeated in the New—if we are free from "the obedience of faith," to use Paul's phrase, because we have been converted—then for exactly the same reason, every justified Old Testament person like Abraham or David was also freed from the Law *on the same basis!* In other words, the Law in the Old Testament never applied to *any* believer in regard to salvation and sanctification, if that is the way we're going to argue. Unbelieving and believing Old Testament men did not need it.

The Law in the Old Testament is the key problem. What was the purpose of the Law in the Old Testament if that previous statement is true? It is quite a problem, because the Law seemed to be, according to Deuteronomy 4:7-8, one of the greatest gifts that God ever gave to His people, or to all mankind for that matter. At least that's the way Moses wrote it. He says in the Deuteronomy passage (which is a sort of sermon upon the Law): "For what nation is there so great, who hath a God so nigh unto them, as the Lord our God is in all things that we call upon him for, and what nation is there so great, that has statutes and judgments so righteous as all this law, which I set before you this day?"

God asserts that the Law is one of His greatest gifts that He has given to His people. On the other hand, if He gave the Law to men, but they are not bound by it because they've been justified and they've been taken out from under the onus of it, then the question naturally arises: "To whom did He give it then? And for what purpose did He give it?"

In the Law of the Lord, Israel was to delight day and night (Ps. 1:2), to meditate on it. Well, why meditate on it if they were freed from it? I mean "free" on the basis of being freed from the moral aspects of the Law as Old Testament believers. The same thing is noted in Psalm 40:8, where it speaks of the Law of the Lord being a great delight. It wasn't a curse; rather, it was a blessing if you listen to what the psalmist proclaimed.

Even in the New Testament, obedience to our Lord is not just an optional spiritual luxury of the Christian life. Much confusion on this point is attributed wrongly to both Testaments. There were no options about knowing, believing, and obeying God then, nor are there now.

There seems to be the erroneous idea that Christianity is like a basic insurance policy. Straight, ordinary life is to raise your hand and say "yes" to the following basic creeds about Christ, or to say, "O.K. if you believe these, you're in." This is "straight life." I must wonder about the reality and validity of these "conversions." Isn't this kind of acceptance just as true of the demons mentioned in James 2:19? They believe, at least intellectually. And I have to wonder how come they're not making it, if that is how Christians allegedly come to possess eternal life.

Actually, the demons believe so firmly that they shake. That's good belief—believing the whole business. But what is wrong with their belief is that it's only an intellectual acceptance. It has nothing to do with the commitment of themselves!

I remember someone who once told me that he didn't like it when I used the word "commitment." It sounded too much like an undertaker's word, or something that the preacher says at the graveside. But perhaps that's not a bad analogy after all. Because it's what I am trying to say. In full commitment, there is a turning over of one's self completely; but instead of entrusting yourself to the earth, you entrust yourself to the living God. The analogy goes further, for we are called upon to die to self, to sin, but to be alive to God.

Others say, "But you don't understand. We've got this super special plan for people who are going to be missionaries, preachers, teachers, or pastors' wives. The whole bit. We've got this super plan, so in case you die on the mission field, or in case you're hung in effigy by students, there's double indemnity. You are a super-saint because you've committed yourself 100 percent to the living God."

I fail to find such a contract. Read through the Scriptures and see people calling upon Him, as in Romans 10:9 and 10, where they believe not only with their hearts but with their mouths, confessing Jesus Christ as Lord. As a matter of fact, the Scripture says: "For to this end, Christ both died, and rose . . . that he might be Lord both of the dead and living" (Rom. 14:9). He wants to be our "Boss." It's ineffective even to use the word "Lord" sometimes because it sounds too sanctified; it has become almost innocuous to both the Christian and the non-Christian community. I used the word "Boss" because it has a little bit of a jolt in it, and all of a sudden we begin to think about it. We should understand that this is precisely what our Lord wants us to do. He wants us to see ourselves in a relationship to Himself as "Boss," to retain the true meaning of "Lord."

In the New Testament, obedience is never optional. In John 14:15 we read: "If ye love me, keep my commandments." There's that big "if," the same word that is found in Exodus 19:5: *"If* ye will obey my voice . . . and keep my covenant [commandments], then ye shall be a peculiar treasure unto me above all people. . . ."

Many people feel that the poor Israelites missed out at this point. They should never have gone for that arrangement. It was a bad deal from the very start. Or as some say, "Israel should have rejected it altogether." But that's not so. The text doesn't actually say that. As a matter of fact, in Deuteronomy 5:29, our Lord says: "O that there were such an heart in them, that they would fear me, and keep all my commandments always, that it might be well with them, and with their children for ever!" Our Lord says in verse 28 of the same chapter, ". . . They have well said all that they have spoken." They had done well to accept the covenant arrangement with God.

If I as a mere man say that they did wrong, I set myself in opposition to God. He said, *"They did well!"* Notice also John 15:10, "If ye keep My commandments, ye shall abide in my love." And read John 3:12, where we find another one of the "ifs." Then turn to Hebrews 3:7 and 8: ". . . if ye will hear his voice, harden not your hearts, as in the provocation, in the day of temptation in the wilderness." The careful reader recognizes that the "if" in these passages is not conditional in the sense that God will be overruled in an option where man's obedience is not forthcoming. Rather, it is speaking of the individual benefits of the full blessing of the gospel, which can come to any person as he lets the Word of God help him grow in sanctification and maturation.

Let us look at the three aspects of the Law. Or is it true that we have three aspects of the Law? Notice that it isn't three different Laws. The Scripture itself does not say that we have a ceremonial Law, a civil Law, and a moral Law. But I think that as the single body can be divided into many members while it is still one, so we can take the Law and see various members and various aspects of it.

But how can I be sure that this one Law of God is divided into three different aspects? Isn't this just a ruse to bring Christians back into bondage to at least part of the Sinaitic legislation? No. We have no less an authority than that of Jesus Himself. He teaches us that there are heavier and lighter matters in the Law (Matt. 23:23). That heavier part can be defined. Jesus says it is the same as that taught by the prophets: "justice, mercy and faith" (cf. Mic. 6:6-8). The same message was given by Jesus in Matthew 9:13 and 12:5-7. Instead of asking Him questions on the ceremonial Law, they should go home and learn what the prophet Hosea meant when he said in 6:6, "I desire mercy, and not [just] sacrifice. . . ." Therefore we can see that Jesus can divide the Law and rank it in accordance with its heavier and lighter parts.

In naming the heavier part, I would suggest the moral aspect of the Law. This one is permanent and eternal since it is grounded in the character of God and reflects His being in Law. The lighter aspects we usually name descriptively as the civil aspect and the ceremonial aspect. These are derivative in nature and temporally conditioned by remarks in passages like Exodus 25:9, 40, which say that the tabernacle is only a "pattern" of the real in heaven. So also argues Hebrews 10:1.

The ceremonial aspect, then, has at least three strands: the tabernacle, which is found in Exodus 25–40; the sacrificial system, which is found in Leviticus 1–7; and the uncleanness and purification aspect, which is found in Leviticus 8–11. We can basically understand the tabernacle. And I want to say something about the sacrificial system later in this chapter. But the third strand of the ceremonial Law—uncleanness and purification—concerns us here. Thus we consider the Law and sanctification.

When we speak about uncleanness, we must remember that uncleanness does not necessarily mean something that is dirty or something that is forbidden. Many unclean things and unclean experiences are unavoidable, involving such experiences as birth and death. Instead, "clean" in this section means being sanctified for service to the living God. A "clean" person is not an "hygienic" person. He is one who is prepared or qualified for service to God.

Cleanliness is a prerequisite to holiness, but not in the sense that we use the little phrase, "cleanliness is next to godliness." That cliché is good, and it has some fine points to it. But that is not what the text is saying here. In Leviticus 8–11, it is speaking about qualification for the worship of a holy God.

Next, consider the civil aspect of the Law. There are aspects in which morality, as given in the Bible, applies to social situations. There are decisions that were given for the judges to use, that closely parallel six other law codes that have been discovered in the Near East dating from ancient times. It is the milieu of that day being reflected, not only in the Word of God and written by Moses, but also known from the time of the Flood, when men came off the ark and were exposed to the revelation of God to Noah. There was a stage when all men knew the grace of God and yet refused to retain it in their knowledge, according to Romans 1 and 2.

Perhaps this is the reason, in part, for the similarity in the various law codes as they have come down to us still preserved, such as the Hammurabi Law Code, the Assyrian Law Code, and the Hittite Law Code.

One comment on this civil aspect of the Law: when it says in Exodus 21 that these are "judgments" or that these are "decisions," notice that the text says that they are to be exercised not by individuals but by the judges. Take, for example, the one in the Bible that is so troublesome to many of us, the *Lex Talionis* law, which many claim to mean that a man may take an eye for an eye and a tooth for a tooth. You and I could get into a rather ridiculous situation if you knocked out my tooth. Then I could put my hand on your shoulder and say, "Hold still," and then try to get one of your teeth.

But this was not the point of that Law at all. It was a sort of stereotype formula which was to be used by the judges in passing judgment. It was trying to guard against inequality in justice. It was intended to make the punishment fit the crime, but no more than that. In application the *Lex Talionis* law helped prevent acts of revenge and counterrevenge in intertribal hostilities, which tended to increase in intensity. Equality of justice is both an Old Testament and a New Testament principle.

Then there is the moral aspect of the Law, which I believe is found mainly in the Ten Commandments and in the holiness teaching in Leviticus 12–22 as well as in Deuteronomy 1–11. The standard of ethics here is as high as it can be. They were told to be holy, because the Lord their God was holy. "Be ye holy, for the Lord your God is holy." How much higher could a man in the Old Testament go in regard to his ethics? He could go no higher, for since the standard was the holiness of the living God, he was urged to match that level. The appeal to match this high level is also presented in Matthew 5:48, "Be ye . . . perfect, even as your Father which is in heaven is perfect!"

Here is one of the principles of Law that I would suggest as a basis of determining which aspects are temporary and which aspect of the Law is permanent because it reflects the very nature of God. His nature is constant, not only for this age but for all the ages to come. Indeeed He is from eternity to eternity. God will never change, and therefore those things that are based on His nature, such as His holiness, will always stay the same. God will never shrink, nor will His standards of righteousness and holiness go up or down. They will be reflected permanently in the moral Law.

There are, however, also those things that are true because they are spoken by our Lord, but they still can be temporary. Such are the ceremonial and civil aspects of the Law. These are validated because they are based upon the Word of God, but when God Himself says that He has instituted something else, something "better," then we have good reason and good cause to go to the next thing that He has taught us.

Look at the moral aspects of the Law. The emphasis here falls on the Law given and on His relationship with His people. This relationship antedates any institution of the command. For instance, look at Exodus 20:2, where He dares to identify Himself as "I am the Lord thy God." This is best demonstrated as He called Moses to leadership over His people. Moses first balked and then tried to excuse himself. What did God say? "Stop chattering, Moses. Keep silent. I'm going to be there; what are you worried about? I will be there to effectively help you in that situation."

Later, in the giving of the Law, He announced Himself as the Lord not only, but also as the Lord God of Israel. In Exodus 20:2, He described Himself as the Lord who brought them out of the land of Egypt. So here is a relationship that had already been established. He referred to this in Exodus 2:24; 6:2-5, where He said in effect, "I will maintain my covenant. I will keep My covenant which I made with you." He was not instituting a new covenant. He was only going to continue that covenant, that promise theme, which already had been initiated.

Furthermore, the context of the Ten Commandments is in the environment of grace. That is, we are in the environment of a relationship that already exists. Those men were not trying to establish fellowship with God. They already had it. He was their Lord. He was their God, their Redeemer, who had brought them out of the land of Egypt. So grace is always in the foreground. And, in Exodus 33:19 and 34:6, 7, He identified Himself as the gracious God, the God who is abundant in mercy and goodness and longsuffering and truth.

May I remind you that all this also is true in connection with the giving of the Ten Commandments. We see it when Moses came down the second time from the mountain, in Exodus 33:19 and 34:6, 7. God proved Himself to be the God who is gracious, abundant in mercy and goodness, who is longsuffering, who is full of lovingkindness and truth. God will be full of truth and grace to those who need it. This is the environment of grace. Indeed, these are the very words used in John 1:17 to describe our Lord Jesus: He came in grace and truth.

"But," you say, "it's not the Lawgiver, nor is it what you say about grace that upsets me. It's the form of the Law. I really react to 'don'ts,' and the Law is mainly in the negative form. This upsets me! Isn't this the opposite to grace?"

On the contrary. I call your attention to the fact that whereas the laws of the Ten Commandments are mostly negative, this is only so because it is much easier to express in a few words what a believer can't do, since he has been freed in the Man of Promise in the Old Testament, or since he has been freed in Christ as the New Testament word would put it. It is far easier to express in a few words the limitations that have been placed upon us, than to open up all the vistas that now are available to us in the freedom which is to be found in Christ Jesus our Lord. Imagine trying to write all the "do's" that the Christian can enter into. The world could not contain the books!

When an evil like murder is prohibited (and indeed the sixth commandment should be translated, "thou shalt not murder"), it does not just mean that we should abstain from injuring or desiring to injure our brother or our neighbor. Also, it means that we are obliged, as I understand this commandment (and as I understand the explication of it through the rest of the Pentateuch and the Prophets) to do all that is within our power to protect our neighbor's life. Contrary to the contemporary concept, we must get "involved."

All avenues of love, therefore, which contribute to the life of our neighbor are to be used. I do not fulfill this law merely by inactivity. That would be equal to not keeping the commandment. It would be equal to death. To do nothing is to die. The Law desires of me something more, some sort of commitment. And it says I should actively seek out and help and aid all those who are in need and those who are close to me.

Notice also, that all moral law is double sided. It makes no difference whether it is stated negatively or positively. Every time we decide to do something in the moral realm, it becomes in the very same moment a refusal to do the opposite. We refuse to take one option, and we opt to take the other. So there always remains in every moral decision what some people refer to as the "agonizing yes and no." There is something that you reject; there is something that you accept. Therefore the negative form is not that large a consideration, since the positive can be stated just as well—and indeed is found in many sections of the Law.[3] Similarly the commandments themselves, or "the ten words," which is the Biblical phrase for them, speak basically about God, and they also speak about our relationship to each other.

First of all, there is the sanctity of God's Person, both in internal and external worship. God is to have no one to rival Him in our hearts. *No one, no thing,* in heaven or in earth is to rival Him in our worship.

That does not just mean that we should not bring in icons and set them up and say, "This is the Lord," or, "This is one of His helpers." Rather, this gets down to how a man worships God. It speaks about everything, everything from the matter of dull, yawning prayers to the matter of posture, and whatever else I expect from God when I go to His house to worship. This is implicit here. Worship is not just a "come as you like it" affair. We come to meet with the living God, and whether it is in private devotions or corporate worship together in a chapel or in a church, the text calls forth from us not only a refusal to bring icons and set them up, but it also asks: "What is your internal state? What is your external state? How much sleep did you get last night? How do you expect to worship the living God if you are tired and exhausted and inattentive because of your own 'busyness'?"

Wouldn't we try to get a good night's rest if we were going to meet the president the next day? Wouldn't there be some attempt within our own being to be at our tip-top best? Well, we're going to meet the King of kings, the King above all the governors and the kings and the presidents of all the earth. Don't you think this calls for an external sort of response, as well as internal? This is the type of thing that the commandment is getting at.

The Law goes on in the third commandment to speak of the sanctity of God's name, which doesn't just mean He is against swearing and "cussing." Some people feel that they have never gotten into trouble with God because they have never violated that commandment, if it just means swearing. But the text doesn't mean that. It means much, much more. God's Name is His reputation.

---

3. A more detailed argument is found in Ezekiel Hopkins, "Understanding the Ten Commandments," in *Classical Evangelical Essays in Old Testament Interpretation,* ed. Walter C. Kaiser, Jr. (Grand Rapids: Baker Book House, 1972), pp. 41-58.

God's Name is His character. God's Name is His doctrine. To use God's Name is to speak of all that God is, and all that He stands for. Many people use the Name of God too lightly. "In vain" actually means "for no purpose."

When I take upon myself the Name of God in holy worship, or I try to do some work in the church in the Name of God, and I do it lightly, with no purpose, then I violate that commandment. I believe this. I think I have run afoul of what that commandment says by using God's Name for no purpose.

Perhaps when I lead in prayer I use the name of the Lord as a comma, a pause, while I'm thinking of my next phrase. This is so common, especially in our evangelical circles, where we often use extemporary prayer. We can interject the Lord's Name so frequently that we can be using it "for no purpose." When it does not form any grammatical function in that sentence, then it is in vain. We are like the heathen. That's what this commandment teaches. There is also much more here, and the Church has to get back to a realization of what our Lord said. She *needs* to know what our Lord said. We need to know the sanctity of God's Name.

We also need to know the sanctity of God's time. The fourth commandment is ceremonial in part because it specifies the seventh day, but it is also moral in part because it says in effect, "God has a right to my time." He gave me time. He gave me life. He has a right to have it back—a right to have it back in rest and a right to have it back in service to Himself. Thus He has set up this symbol, even within the creative order. A day for God is not too much to ask. It is not only healthy spiritually, it is also healthy physically and emotionally.

In the fifth commandment there is the sanctity of God's representatives, not only of father and mother, but through the whole of life's relationships: parent-child relationship, a governed relationship, student council-student body relationship, and teacher-student relationship. These all come together and are part of the representative plan of God. God has representatives here and He asks that we honor them. We should honor them because they belong to a pattern that He has put within society. This pattern is to be found in the institution of the family, in the institution of marriage, and in the institution of the state.

In the sixth commandment there is the sanctity of life. Life is so precious, and the Church ought to be more conscious of this than anyone else. Do we realize that probably more than at any other time in the history of the world, people are being slaughtered at an alarming rate? I don't just mean wars and uprisings, though these conditions are also involved. But what about on our highways? What about our abortion laws? We've got to speak out if, in the view of the Biblical text, a baby when conceived in the womb is itself considered to be life. To have an abortion is to take a life.

The commandments talk about the sanctity of marriage. God thought it was so important that it was the first institution that He gave to man after He created him in the Garden of Eden.

There is also the sanctity of property.

And there is the sanctity of truth. And how I wish I could show this is presently under attack. For many years evangelicals have been accused as people who were slipshod in their academic methods. They were labeled as people who wanted just "to get the blessing" but didn't want to get the truth. They were supposed to be anti-intellectual snobs. But a massive cultural attack on truth has happened in our day, in this very decade in which we are living. Probably before the decade is out, the last stronghold of truth anywhere to be found will not be in the universities; it will be rather in the backwaters, in the outposts of our culture, in the evangelical schools, among those who were once accused of hiding from the truth at its academic and intellectual level. How wrong was that accusation.

There has been a tremendous pressure upon young people who have come through the public school education system for twelve or thirteen years. Perhaps they were already brainwashed through the mass media of communication. Through education and media they learn that truth is relative. We must understand the tension produced because of the dialectic that says, "Not yes or no, but maybe,"—that there is always some grey in between. That is the Hegelian dialectic, which was born in another day but now has come to full fruition in our present decade.

Finally there is the primacy of the intent—the primacy of the heart, as the last commandment says: "Thou shalt not covet." It was here that Paul felt his defeat as a man. He said, "I was doing fine on commandments one through nine, until I found number ten (cf. Rom. 7:7). And that was too bad. Because that tenth one said that I should go back through all the earlier commandments again and see that it was also a matter of the internal heart attitude of man."

That is precisely what Jesus said in the Sermon on the Mount. It wasn't just the outward act of adultery—it was also the act of committing it in one's heart. It wasn't just the act of murder—it was also the act of hate. That is what our Lord was highlighting. He said: "It hath been said . . . but I say unto you." Some people think that our Lord said, "You have seen it written, but I say unto you." That's not what He said at all. He said, "You hear the other fellows teaching, don't you? You hear what they're saying, don't you?" As a matter of fact, there are passages in Matthew where He even quotes what is being said by others, and there is not one scrap of Old Testament basis for it. In Matthew 5:43, for example, Jesus said, "You have heard it said . . . hate your enemy." The Old Testament never said that. It said the reverse!

Now for the conclusion. There is wonderful provision for failure, through the forgiveness that follows. It is startling to realize that the very Law that held up such a high standard also made provision for men who fail. I once thought that the Law had no such provisions at all. That once the Law was broken, you were out. To disobey just once; to fail the condition just once—that was it. That proved that the Law could not be kept. How wrong I was.

Instead of the Law saying that lawbreakers would forfeit their relationship with God, that same Law provided a means of fellowship. What a thrill to realize this great truth! This is "shouting" ground! For whereas it held up the high standards of God, and God did not lower His standard of righteousness, He put grace in. He put "giftiness" in to help us come up to meet the standard, to reach the place of fellowship with Him.

God kept the standard high, then He gave men the ability, His ability, to meet that standard. How does this come about? Just as fellowship was conditional on faith in the promise doctrine, so here it is sustained by forgiveness. Lawbreakers can be forgiven men. The Law was no more conditional than the promise was conditional. In Genesis 26:5, it says, *"Because . . . Abraham obeyed . . . my commandments, my statutes, and my laws."* "Because" is emphasized simply because of Exodus 19:5, where it is also emphasized. It is the promise continuing on into the Law.

An illustration, for instance, can be "righteous Noah" (cf. Genesis 7:1) or "a righteous Lot." Imagine that! Lot was a rascal, yet II Peter 2:7 and 8 speaks of how a *righteous Lot* vexed his *righteous soul.* "Righteous" Lot! How did he get righteous? He seemed to entirely miss what we would term righteousness.

The greatest ceremony in the whole of the Pentateuch, actually the high point, comes in Leviticus 16, the Day of Atonement. What a terrific picture. The priest makes atonement for himself. He takes off his beautiful robes and his vestments, and he takes on the humble linen cloth, which speaks of the humiliation of the man and the loneliness of the man as well. Everyone else must be out of the tabernacle. He must go into the holy place, then the holy of holies by himself once a year. And what is he doing this for? Leviticus 16:5 says that he is doing it for a "sin offering."

The sin offering has two parts, for there are two goats that are brought for a sin offering. It's very important to note: *two* goats for *one* sin offering. And what is to be done with the two goats? First the priest must make atonement for himself. He is not the sinless Christ. He is a man who must be forgiven before he can intercede and mediate on behalf of other men. This was not so with our Lord. But it was necessary for this man, the priest. True, he humbled himself, and he put on a linen robe as did our Lord. But this man had to provide a sacrifice for himself. The sinless Christ did not need a sacrifice. He was the sacrifice Himself.

So the man, having provided sacrifice for himself while the congregation waited breathlessly outside, then came out and cast lots to see which of the two goats should be killed. He placed his hand (this is terribly important, too) on the head of that one goat and confessed over it "all the sins of Israel." He confessed *all* of their sins! In effect, that goat was taking the sins of all the people on its head. The priest would then kill the goat and take it in to the place of atonement, taking the blood into the place of the mercy seat.

What happened? It was the means of "at-one-ment" with God and man. The word "atonement" was created for theology. It meant "at-one-ment," or "God and man at one." How do they come together as one? Through the blood! Just red and white corpuscles? No, no, that's not the important thing. It is the death of the victim acting as a substitute. In medical practice they say that blood is equal to a transfusion, the impartation of life. That is not so here. This is life spilt out. This is life given up in death, and it is death in a sacrificial manner. It speaks of the death of Christ which was to come.

Thus the means of atonement was by the shedding of blood. Having done this, the priest came out, and once again (notice this, it's so important) he confessed the sins of the people over the second goat. Why? Because he could not resurrect the first goat. He could not bring it to life again. Thus there was one ceremony with two parts, but they both belonged to the same ceremony. A dead sacrifice, a living sacrifice.

The second goat over which he also confessed the sins of all Israel, was led away out of the camp. A man was designated to take it out to make sure it got lost, forever gone. Why? Because sins were not only forgiven by the blood of the animal substituted for the sinners until the perfect God-Man should come and die for all men once for all, but according to the Old Testament, they were also forgotten. They were removed as far as the east is from the west, according to Psalm 103. They were taken away forever.

Thus the children of Israel had their sins forgotten as well as forgiven. Christians know that the Lord has forgiven them. Do they also remember that the Lord also *forgets* the sins that have been confessed to Him? So many people carry around a tremendous load. They have forgotten that those sins are not only forgiven, but forgotten as well. In fact they would have to remind God about them. He has forgiven and forgotten them! The means of the atonement is by the shedding of blood. The effect of the atonement is the removal of guilt.

Just one last thing: How many sins are forgiven and forgotten, according to Leviticus 16:21? *All* the sins! Was this an external act only? No. According to verse 29, they were to "afflict their souls," and the atonement was only efficacious subjectively if the individual confessed and truly repented of his own sins. Repentance is necessary for confession and forgiveness. And we should put that back into our personal witnessing, too, when we seek to lead men to Christ. Repentance is a tremendously important point.

What then is atonement in the Old Testament? Are my sins covered? Oh, no, they are more than covered. They are removed. What does atonement mean? Simply that I have been ransomed by a substitute. And in all the 100 times in which the verb occurs in the Old Testament, it means the man has received release from sins because a substitute has been provided. Indeed this is the means provided by the Law itself.[4] And in it are the paths of life.

4. The best development of this theme I have ever read is in a sermon preached on Tuesday morning, March 18, 1856, at Saint Margaret's Church, Lothbury, England, by Henry Melvill, "The Jewish and Christian Sacrifices" in *The Preacher in Print*, Second Series, *The Golden Lectures* (London: James Paul, 1856), pp. 57-64.

# 4

# The Historian's Outlook

## Interpretation of the Past and Future

History is not always interesting to the casual student. But for the Christian student, who sees God in all history, it is a living subject, not a dead past. History has been called "His Story." It is really God who controls history. The one thing that is impressed on the Bible student of the two Testaments is that in both the so-called secular and the theological, or sacred, domains of history, God is the One who is in charge.

Do you realize how many references there are within the sacred text to the fact that God controls the history of other peoples, while at the same time He is directing it for His "theological" purposes? This is true particularly for the people of Israel. In Amos 9:7 God says that He not only brought the Israelites out of the land of Egypt, but He also controlled all the other exoduses (or exodii!) of the nations. However we describe these "goings out," there were a number of them. He brought the Syrians up from Kir. He brought the Philistines up from Caphtor. In that same list the Ethiopians are also mentioned. And this is the same God that brought Israel up out of the land of Egypt!

God is the One who favored all nations. In Deuteronomy 2:9, 12, and 19, He says that those nations of Trans-Jordania: Moab, Edom, Ammon, all received their countries from His hand, just as Israel had received Canaan. God had previously run the former inhabitants out of that territory because the cup of their iniquity was filled up. Then He moves His people and other peoples in.

God holds the same yardstick, the same measure of righteousness over all nations. And He requires the same degree of holiness on the part of all people.

In due time, the "great Emim" who lived there, and the "tall Anakim" who had formerly lived there, and the "giant Zamzum-mims" who had lived there before that (these are all mentioned in

71

Deuteronomy 2) were all driven out because of their wickedness, which was very great.

In like manner, the land was given to Israel. Therefore Israel's conquest of Palestine was not just a matter of divine favoritism, but God ran the whole world by these same principles.

The same principle of "exodus" holds true today. God, after many generations, and sometimes after many millennia, moves among the nations with both long-term and short-term credits of mercy. When a people, regardless of whether they are a so-called Christian nation or not, have their "cup of iniquity filled up," then God moves in judgment against them. The prophetic message for all who declare the Word of God and teach the Word of God, is to proclaim that there is a "doomsday" coming for that people. God will wipe them out, push them out, or bring them down to the dust. As Mrs. Billy Graham once very appropriately and theologically said, "God will have to apologize to Sodom and Gomorrah if He does not visit the United States in judgment." For surely, the cup of iniquity is coming dangerously close to being filled up in America, too. In fact, all of our Western civilization had better beware. We are running low on divine credit and high on compounded wickedness.

Given our present course, judgment is sure, and anyone who does not preach with that kind of distinctiveness, with that feeling for the prophetic Word of God, does not know the God of history, who is represented in both Testaments.

Let me add this: the "scandal" of the Biblical faith is its historical character. If it weren't for the Bible's historical character, many people would "buy" Christianity. We could sweep literally thousands, perhaps millions, of people into the Christian faith, especially in a day when the world has adopted so much of the Eastern Oriental philosophical mentality. But in tying this whole matter into history, the Biblical message has become an offense, or as Paul calls it, "the offense of the cross."

People prefer, by the psyche or by the subjective processes, to steal into the divine presence through some pantheistic way, if they could. But the "scandal" of Biblical faith is that it took place in our kind of geography and history. God came, and was made in the likeness and in the form of man. He took upon Himself human flesh. He came at the midpoint of all history, and so speaks to all history. It is "His Story" indeed!

Will Herberg[1] says that Biblical faith is also historical, not merely because it *has* history, or deals *with* historical events (there's nothing particularly novel in that), but it is historical in a much more profound sense because *it is itself* history. The message that Biblical faith proclaims, the judgments it pronounces, the salvation it promises, the teaching it communicates; these are all defined historically and are understood as historical realities. This does not make it offensive to us, since it helps to humanize it, to bring it down to our level where we can understand it and where we can (as we say today) "identify" with it. To de-historicize history or to de-historicize Biblical faith is like trying to paraphrase poetry. You ruin it. You just take all that is good and meaningful out of it. It is no longer poetry.

In the same way, if we try to take the historical aspect out of Biblical faith, we have not created a better situation in which a person can believe. We have only evaporated the main content of the gospel. We have taken out the bulwark that was put there. Hence, the current dilemma found in scholarly circles with the "faith-history tension" is wrongly placed. It is once again a case where our culture has invaded the Christian faith. We cannot accept an acculturation of Biblical faith, which is really transcultural. But neither can we accept faith devoid of its historical roots and consciousness.

Herberg went on to give the view heathenism had of man and his relationship to God, where he made all of reality to be nature. For him the thing that was real was nature itself, and in the context of nature, man struggled to both find himself and establish meaning. Today we do not seem to be so far from that same position. Perhaps we shouldn't throw stones at heathenism, because even scientific naturalism says that nature is ultimate and that man is just a biological organism adjusting to this environment.

Greek philosophy and Oriental mysticism is a second option opened to man for the understanding of himself and his relationship to God or to the ultimates in the universe. Many think that these two systems are diverse, but there are some things that are very, very common between Greek philosophy and Oriental mysti-

---

1. The basic structure and content of the three ways to regard history are in Will Herberg, "Biblical Faith as Heilsgeschichte," *Christian Scholar* 39 (1956): 25-29.

cism. They both say that the ultimately real, the basic building block of the whole universe, is the timelessly eternal that is behind nature. They deny appearances. Anything that has to do with "stuff"—with matter, or material—is to be put in one pile. So the temporal, the material, the empirical, and the multiple, is all put on one side. That pile is useless. Then they put on the other side the spiritual, the eternal, the immutable, and the singular. And that is very good. It is almost as if they were saying: "Here you have that 'other' world, and here you have the 'good' world."

All this contributed to the Gnostic heresy, where the Gnostics (particularly as John opposes it in his First Epistle) feel that to be released from the body, like a blithe spirit to go flying off somewhere else, is the epitome of one's salvation. Quite frankly that doesn't appeal to me at all. I do have problems with the flesh. But I am going to see this "stuff" resurrected and changed. It has its foibles, but it is made by God, and it is stamped, as it were, with the label, "Made by God." Made in His image! And this "stuff" is going to be resurrected.

I am really interested in continuing to exist as a person in a body. I can't think of myself without my body. I, like Paul in II Corinthians 5, somewhat cringe at the state of being without my body, although I, too, with him say, "Far better to be present with the Lord and to be abroad from my body, than to be in my body and to be abroad from my Lord." But if I had my "druthers," I would rather be with my body and with the Lord, thank you! And that's what I think Paul says there, too. I'd just as soon have both, and who would not? That's the wonderful thing about the resurrection itself.

No, you Greek philosophers and you Oriental mystics, you've got it all wrong. We want to take both of these things here. Don't you know God made the world? Don't you know God made this body "stuff"? Don't you know that everything you can see and feel and touch belongs to my Lord? Don't you know He will win it back to Himself once more? What are we trying to do, just save souls, those things that float around like ectoplasm? No, God will change everything in redeeming the world back to Himself.

What about Biblical faith as a third option? Biblical faith says both nature and time are real. They're not illusory; they are gifts of God. They are part of His creation. Man cannot be dissolved into nature, as heathenism would have it. Nor can man be dissolved into a kind of timeless spirit as mysticism would have him do. Our Lord speaks in His Biblical revelation to men in their totality. At present He saves in part. But one day when He shall come back, and we shall see Him face to face, the whole created order itself will be taken to Himself. And man, this historical being who can and does have a history, has also a real body (and thus is part of nature) with a real personality, freedom, and self-awareness by virtue of being in the image of God.

So that's the "faith-history tension." It has manifested itself in our time, particularly through that interesting fellow, Rudolf Bultmann. He maintains that the historical method includes the presupposition that history is a unity in the sense of a closed continuum of the facts. This closedness means that the continuum of historical happenings cannot be rent by the interference of the supernatural or by transcendent power. Do you accept that? I don't. I don't accept it at all. The Bible tells me that "the earth is the Lord's and the fulness thereof." What happens here is the result of His work, and He Himself is able to come within the continuum, and even interrupt this world of history for His own purposes.

Neither can I accept the dictum of Lessing, that the incidental truths of history can never become the proof of the necessary truths of reason. Because as soon as I do that, I become involved in the whole subjectivistic thing which, as a Christian, I hate with deep passion. It violently divides the world God has put together.

I would urge you to investigate it, and to make sure you don't fall for the same thing, that "Kirkegaardian leap of faith" that says, "Here I am; I will close my eyes, for I am going to jump."

I just ask one thing of our modern jumper, "Where are you going to jump?"

Perhaps he would say, "I don't know, I'm just going to jump."

"Why?"

"Because I've got to believe, I've got to believe."

But I protest, "How do you know who or what to believe? On what basis do you make your leap? Blind believism is not Biblical belief." Someone has said that belief is accepting something, or putting one's trust in something, for which there are no reasons. But if you are going to put your trust in something for which there are no reasons, that is not faith. You've misspelled the word. That is folly! And that's not too simple a definition.

You ask someone, "Did you buy a car?"

"Oh yes, I bought a car."

"Well, is it in good condition? Does it run smoothly?"

"I don't know. I haven't seen it."

"Well, does it have good tires on it?"

"Now, that's a good question. I bought it on faith."

"You mean you have no idea how good the tie rods are, or anything else about it?"

"I don't have any idea."

"What sort of car is it?"

"I don't know. I just bought the whole thing on faith. It was a good deal and I took it."

What the car buyer is saying is, "I really believed." But I say that he is not a believer—he is a fool! He bought it on folly, not on faith. Biblical faith wants to examine its reasons, and the greatest reasons that our Lord Jesus Christ Himself gave were His works. Our Lord said, "Believe Me. But if you can't believe Me for My words' sake [perhaps you are, as they say, "from Missouri" and you cannot and will not believe until you have seen it, touched it, and heard it], then believe Me for My works' sake." And His works are the works of history.

But let us turn back to some of the rough problems of history, such as those we find in Genesis 1 and 11. This is the so-called "primeval history." How often have we been told that these chapters are not part of the historical continuum? Let me get one point across. We must—not only as Biblical interpreters, but also as people of the Book who are trying to exercise good procedure and methodology—at least endeavor to repeat what the writers themselves have said.

We have not fulfilled our job until we have let the writer speak for himself. Some people may disagree, particularly in a non-evangelical audience. I say to them, isn't it fair to take any book on its own terms first of all? Isn't it only fair to look at what the author is trying to say? Wouldn't we do that for Homer? Wouldn't we do that for Thucydides? Shouldn't we do that for any ancient piece of literature? Then why not for the Bible?

So I am taking what I assume to be a legitimate approach to any type of literature. Notice what the writer of this material says. And since we are looking at the Bible as literature, although it is more than literature, let us take those chapters of Genesis in the context of the whole fifty chapters of the book. There we find ten recurring phrases that are repeated throughout the Book of Genesis. These phrases actually supply us with an outline for the Book of Genesis. For instance, we read: "These are the generations of"; or "the book of the generations of"; and these words are repeated ten times (Gen. 2:4; 5:1; 6:9; 10:1; 11:10, 27; 25:12; 19; 36:1; [36:9 text?]; 37:2). They are probably used as headings; not just as colophons, or ornamental touches at the end of the sections.

Notice that six times the writer used that phrase in the first eleven chapters, and four times in Genesis 12–50. That second part of Genesis is in the patriarchal narrative. Now, one thing we have learned from recent archaeology, which we will discuss later, is that the patriarchal history is probably one of the best documented accounts in the Old Testament as far as current research and writing is concerned. There are two high spots in present-day archaeology. One is the period of time dealing with the patriarchs (the Middle Bronze Age of 2000-1500 B.C.); and the other one is the inter-Testamental period with the Dead Sea Scrolls. And these are almost at the two opposite ends of the Old Testament canon.

Fortunately we have had great quantities of material from those two sources. It is interesting, too, that many people who denied the authenticity or the general authenticity of the patriarchal history, are the same people who went out into the field and dug up the artifacts and epigraphic materials. It was not an evangelical or a conservative who was there and dug them up. Nor were they evangelicals who demonstrated the reliability of them. They were men who were not committed to our theological position. We only jumped on the bandwagon after they had started it all.

But to return to the issues at hand, it was the discoveries of archaeology that bolstered a sagging scholarly confidence in the patriarchal narrative of Genesis. My point is that the writer of Genesis conceived of the status of chapters 1–11 as having the same historical reliability as the second half of the book, and presented these earlier chapters with the same sort of literary format as he did chapters 12–50. Therefore, we should accord Genesis 1–11 the same standing as Genesis 12–50, since the author indicated that he meant both sections to be taken as historical. In fact, that phrase which appears ten times can be translated, "the histories of. . . ." This can be well demonstrated. It is a factual piece of information.

When I was in a public high school, I was taught the point of view that Genesis, particularly chapters 1 and 2, were poetical narrative. I now know that this view was mere wishful thinking, and that the wish was parent to the thought. The truth of the matter is that it is straightforward prose. Anyone who has had just a smattering of Hebrew can see that the point is very, very plain. The status of those first two chapters is straightforward prose.

Then someone comes up and says, "Really, you don't have an appreciation for it. There really is a myth behind it, a myth of the Babylonian story. You must understand that the Babylonian myth of creation is really the story from which our Hebrew account came." And they say this is indicated by one little word, or at least principally by one little word, the Hebrew word for "deep." That word is *tehom*. *Tehom* is supposed to be a weak reflection of a Babylonian goddess by the name of Tiamat.

Now you can see there is really a slight difference of spelling there. You may wonder about the "h," which is a real problem, requiring a very difficult explanation for the protagonist of that point of view. It is difficult to see how that letter can get into the middle of that word. I am not going to suggest a way, because I don't know of any way in which it got there. The "at" on the end of Tiamat I can explain as a feminine ending. But be that as it may, the story that is told in the Babylonian narrative, as some of you may have read, is a story about the "original" couple—Apsu and Tiamat, "papa and mama" of all the rest of the deities. Then children came along, a brood of young deities, or gods. But like most kids, and especially in a large family, they raised a lot of havoc! Commotion everywhere, and it got under Apsu's skin. (I think skin is the right word!)

At any rate, he decided to take care of the problem, and in typical Near Eastern fashion, the deities, who are capable of almost anything, followed suit here. He got rid of a number of them, and apparently the noise died down. But this left the offspring in somewhat of a lurch. So they formed a rebellion. And this was the first uprising, according to Babylonian history.

Then the offspring gods killed their father god. This presented a sort of Freudian situation. And don't forget, even this type of situation has been grist for Freud's mill. The point then is made that the wife, Tiamat, became somewhat upset at losing her husband. A very "human" reaction. So Tiamat organized a retaliatory force. Meanwhile the gods themselves appointed Marduk as their champion.

Marduk in Babylonian theology is somewhat like Baal in Canaanite theology. And Marduk had a plan. He decided that as soon as Tiamat opened her mouth, they would fill her up with plenty of air until she became quite bloated. The idea then was to throw a dart into her. You know the result. She expired—or, rather, exploded! The story then goes on to tell how they took Tiamat and sliced her in half. One half they arched upward to become the sky; the other half became the earth. And so there is a canopy effect, the original astrodome! Underneath is the flat, terrestrial part—our earth.

The claim is that there is a faint recollection of all this in the Bible, through the use of the same name for the word *deep*. It is a beautiful sort of work, and makes a rather interesting story. But I must say that deep down in the real nitty gritty of the story itself, the details begin to fold up. It is an interesting project to go through historical research, and see how some scholars have implicitly followed the preceding scholar's judgment in these matters. One man footnoted another man—Dr. "So and So"—as a sort of chain reaction.

It has been only recently that someone has dared to question the orthodoxy of that view. At any rate, as it turns out, not only is it philologically impossible to derive *tehom* from *tiamat,* but also the function of the two are quite different in the actual part they play. The word for "deep" has shown itself to be indigenous to the Canaanite culture, and if any borrowing is done, there is a recent article in the *Journal of the American Oriental Society* that shows there is just as good a case for the Babylonians borrowing from the Canaanites, as the converse.[2]

That has been one of the main bases for constructing the case of similarity between the two narratives. The story builds up, until we're told that it's not only this word for "deep" which occurs in Genesis 1:2, but it is also the idea of a three-storied universe. Genesis 1 is supposed to support the idea that there is a triple-

2. Thorkild Jacobsen, "The Battle Between Marduk and Tiamat," *Journal of Oriental Society* 88 (1968):104-8.

decked universe. First there is heaven above, which is a kind of firmament which has holes or slots in it to let the rain and the starlight through. Second, there are pillars that come up and support the flat earth, and third, there's sheol down in the bottom, the abyss, the deep—the water that's under the earth. And so there is "heaven above," "earth beneath," and the "waters under the earth." One, two, three.

The question is whether the Bible actually presents a triple-decked universe. Personally, I contest that point of view. There is not a hard dome over everything according to this Hebrew historian. He has not borrowed a mythological motif at all. Rather, what he talks about is an "expanse." The same word occurs in Ezekiel 1 and 10, and means an expanse that has nothing at all to do with hardness. The idea of "hardness" came through Latin, from which we get our word *firmament*. It also came through Greek, from which we get our word *stereo*. As in stereo sets or stereophonic equipment, there is a *hard* living presence or sound.

But the Hebrew text seems to be very, very plain. It's an expanse. Ezekiel's vision, recorded in his first chapter, speaks of a wheel in the middle of the wheel. Then he speaks of a throne set up, on an "expanse." It's the same word that's used in Genesis 1, and had nothing to do with an astrodome effect, or again, even with its hardness, but only with its extent.

Thus I would deny the three-storied universe, especially when modern, unbelieving scholarship goes on to press the literary figures, and speaks of the four corners of the globe. The Bible speaks of the four corners of the globe, but it doesn't speak of them in term of geographic points, as if this world really is flat. A national news company oftentimes ends up its news broadcast with the boast that the news has been gathered from "the four corners of the earth." We understand what they mean. It's a figure of speech. They have merely said that they've gone out in all directions to get their news.

When we read about "the waters under the earth," it's the Hebrew expression for the shoreline. In Deuteronomy 4:18, we read that that's where the fishermen go for their fish. They must have wonderful sinkers and long lines if they are going all the way down to Sheol to catch their fish! They actually fished in the waters below the shoreline, and that's what is meant by "waters under the earth." This is not something that is way down, but rather a concept of water below the shoreline. Surely they are as entitled to their own cultural expressions as we are to ours.[3]

There are other things to discuss here, such as the chronology of Genesis. Some people have used the genealogies in Genesis 5 and Genesis 11, have even counted them, and have come up with the precise time when Adam was created. Dear Bishop Lightfoot got involved in this method, and he really figured it out quite closely. He settled on October 23 at 9:00 A.M., 45th meridian time, 4004 B.C. That's precision if I've ever heard of it. Someone else very wryly said, "Closer than this, as a cautious scholar, the Vice-Chancellor of Cambridge University did not venture to commit himself!"

But the point is, the last datable item in the Bible that we can put a finger on, is Abraham. That is around 2000 or 2100 B.C. But from there back, the genealogies have a built-in warning signal. They are put together artificially in the sense that ten names were selected in Genesis 5, ten names in Genesis 11, and both of these end with three sons. Noah has three sons; Terah has three sons. The record itself tells us not to add these up, for the simple reason that the Bible itself does not add them up. The Bible gives totals in Exodus 12:40 and in I Kings 6:1, but it does not give totals here. That was not the purpose of the writer in giving the genealogies.

Rather, this is the type of situation we find: Terah was seventy years old and he begat Abram, Nahor, and Haran (Gen. 11:26). Now in reading that, it sounds as though the nurse came out of the O.B. ward and said, "Congratulations, Terah, you have triplets!" And this would be so if they were all born on his seventieth birthday! But then we read, "All the days of Terah were 205" (Gen. 11:32).

Later we read that Abram left Haran after his father died (Gen. 12:4). Check that against Acts 7:4. If Abram left Haran when his father died, how old do you think Terah was if Abram was born on his father's seventieth birthday? It doesn't take much arithmetic to figure that out. Even the new math is not needed here.

---

3. For a more detailed presentation of this case with bibliography, see Walter C. Kaiser, Jr., "The Literary Form of Genesis 1-11" in *New Perspectives in the Old Testament*, ed. J. Barton Payne (Waco: Word Books, 1970), pp. 48-65.

The text says Abram was 75. Well, 75 plus 70 gives 145; it does not give 205. The father must have died on his 145th birthday, not on his 205th. Someone was wrong, unless you understand the use of "begat." It can mean to have one's own son or daughter, to begin having children, or to be the ancestor of some distant future offspring.

Terah begat Abram, Nahor, and Haran. So the text itself has a built-in warning against date setting. If the father was 205, and Abram was 75 years old, then 75 from 205 leaves 130. So 130 was actually Terah's age when Abram was born. We would have made a mistake of 60 years if we had not been watching the text carefully, if we had just counted up the years themselves.

Perhaps someone will say, But how much can you stretch these things? I don't know. I don't have any idea. I do know that there are demonstrable gaps in the Biblical records of as many as seven generations. So the question naturally is asked: what's the function of the number that is recorded in Genesis 5 and 11? If it says that a son was born on his 130th birthday, how does that number function? I think that number will function in some cases by telling us at what age it was that an unnamed descendant was born who became the father of the next important person singled out in the genealogies. The materials for working with such genealogies of the Old Testament is not really modern. It was done by the grand, conservative scholar William Henry Green, in an article "Primeval Chronologies" in *Bibliotheca Sacra* for April 1890. Perhaps it's about time this excellent information got out![4]

The point we are making is that we shouldn't just use the numbers, then add them up, and thus go back and find out precisely when the creation was. I *know* when the creation of the world was. The Bible dates it clearly in Genesis 1:1. It was in *the beginning!* That is the Biblical figure. When was Adam created? Sometime after that. Just how long I can't say with any definiteness because of the way in which the word *yom,* "day," is used in that context. "Day" in that same place means "daylight" as opposed to "nighttime." (See Genesis 1:5.) It means a twenty-four-hour day in verse 14. "And God said, Let there be lights in the

---

4. This article is readily available again in *Classical Evangelical Essays in Old Testament Interpretation,* ed. Walter C. Kaiser, Jr. (Grand Rapids: Baker Book House, 1972), pp. 13-28.

firmament of the heaven to divide the day from the night; and let them be for signs, and for seasons, and for days, and years."

Then in Genesis 2:4, he summarizes the six days of creation, and says: "These are the generations of the heavens and of the earth . . . in the day that the Lord God made the earth and the heavens." We must think in terms of that day, as when we say "the day of the horse and buggy," or, "the day of the phonograph." It is the day in which is gathered together the totality of all the preceding creative acts! Therefore we conclude that the author of Genesis has at his disposal in this very context at least three different meanings for the word *day*.

When we continue on in Genesis, we come to the record of the Tower of Babel. Recent archaeological finds have also established the authenticity of this record. It all rings true like accurate historiographical materials.

There are a great number of names listed in Genesis 1-11. There are also a number of cities mentioned. We find many cultural ideas, all of which can be tested. For example, iron is mentioned in Genesis 4. For a long time everybody said that this is impossible, since the Iron Age in every archaeological scheme begins at 1200 B.C. That is, everybody said so except those that were doing the actual digging. For instance, in Turkey, on two occasions, archaeologists found iron. One was found by the Oriental Institute of Chicago. They dug up the blade and the handle of a knife. They analyzed it, and it turned out to be terrestrial iron! It was made of terrestrial and not meteorite iron. And there's a difference in the nickel content of these two metals. The artisans had dug this from the earth somewhere, and had made it into an iron tool. That one was dated 2500 B.C.

Later, about 1962-64, also in Turkey, archaeologists were digging, and they reported on two other finds of two implements made out of iron, dated by carbon 14 as 5800 and 5500 B.C.! We know that arts, skills, and cultural development can be lost. That's precisely what we have in regard to iron. The historiographer of the Bible is vindicated in his claims by modern archaeology.

Moving on to the patriarchal era, the historians' approach here has been simply fantastic. We have an abundance of tablets with magnificent historical records. Some of the best finds are still being located in the basements of many museums. They have not yet been uncrated. There are thousands of these tablets that have been brought back from digs in the East.

Not only artifacts are being found, but also the epigraphic materials, written on tablets that are so exciting to Biblical historians. It's refreshing to find types of confirmation that respond to such issues as when Abraham is supposed to have visited cities like Shechem, Jerusalem, and Hebron. Now we know that those very cities were in existence.

In Egypt we came across two batches of Execration Texts, a sort of cursing text of the type that was used to put the "hex" on someone. Persons would write a name on little pieces or sherds of pottery which were called "ostracon." Then they would smash them in small pieces and thus "ostracize" the person. It was thought in those simple days, that to break a person's name was to put a spell on him.

Even cities and nations were "ostracized." And what were the cities that they were complaining about in those B.C. years of 1800 and 1900? Shechem and Hebron and Jerusalem, the very ones that Abraham and the patriarchs were visiting!

Look at Biblical customs. Some people say that many of them sound false, contrived, and uncultured. People just don't go around selling their birthrights. Did you ever hear of anyone selling his birthright for some soup, must less anything else? They don't do that now. But they did then. The point is, on one tablet from Nuzi, we find the record of a fellow selling a grove of trees for a certain number of sheep. And the dates are approximately 1600 to 1500 B.C., in the back eddies of Near Eastern culture.

What about the matter of giving handmaids for wedding presents? Today the happy couple is given a washer, not a washerwoman. But in that day, that's precisely what they did, so the tablets show. And so the Bible makes claims for Sarah, Leah, and Rachel.

What did they call children during that time? Today there are names that are "in," which are popular and acceptable. There may be Stephanie, or Rebecca, or Keith. This kind of thing goes in cycles. There are popular names that everyone seems to be using at a particular time. What were they using during the time of the patriarchs? Well, at Mari, in 1800 B.C., it was Benjamin, Zebulun, Joseph, Jacob, or Abraham. Sounds normal, doesn't it? At least for the patriarchal times of Genesis 12–50. The same sort of names that we find in the Biblical text. The history of the Bible is neither false nor superfluous. It is part and parcel of that message and action of God. God spoke through the times and spoke to the times.

What about the whole matter of scientific archaeology? Have we dug up any of these cities mentioned? Here again there are positive results. The point is that the record of the patriarchs has been illuminated in a fantastic number of ways.

But that really doesn't prove anything. You can't go up to a person, push a book on archaeology under his nose and say, "See, see here," and hold your finger on the archaeological find. That person will most likely say that it needs "interpretation." Furthermore, he may also complain in terms like these: "You don't understand. We agree that the finding is valid. But what you were claiming is that the first five books of the Bible were written by Moses. And it's not that way at all."

Our imaginary protagonist says that what really took place was that the events happened back in 2000 to 1800 B.C., but they were handed down by oral tradition for over a millennium, in some cases a millennium and a half, until finally they were written down in 850, 750, 621 and 450 B.C. At last there appears the book which you now think is one book, the Pentateuch. It was finally produced as a whole in 400 B.C. And the "scissors and paste job" on it was done so accurately that most people (at least theologically conservative people) still don't know that it was patched together. Perhaps, it is suggested, if you go to university, you will be able to find the fine, fine edges, and see precisely where the snips were made. Thus the sharp critic might reason it out.

Well, let's investigate it because what he says sounds fair. But oral tradition for a millennium and a half? That is amazing. Can he mean they carried all these idiosyncrasies through the myriads of many generations? Now that is amazing, if not miraculous.

Let us think for a moment of Gospel criticism. Have you ever seen the response of a fellow, perhaps from the same liberal crowd, when someone says the gospel events happened during A.D. 30, but they weren't written down till A.D. 60. Now that is thirty years. But the critic is up on his feet with hands in the air. Why? Evidently the unpardonable sin has just been committed. How can one expect events to be remembered accurately for thirty years? That's too long. Too long? On one hand they agree to a millennium and a half for memories to hold all that detail. But they cannot accept a time lapse of thirty years! I really don't understand this kind of objection.

There is one thing that could reverse the logic of two hundred years of destructive literary criticism. This is seen best in Meredith Kline's work on the vassal treaty.[5] Kline, from Gordon Conwell Divinity School, did some work in 1960 on the vassal treaties that came from both the Hittites and the Esarhaddon. These are variously dated. The Hittite treaties came from the second millennium, and are to be dated about 1500 to 1400 B.C. The Esarhaddon and the Aramaic treaties come from about 800 to 600 B.C.

There is a world of difference between these two, because the standard form for the vassal treaty in the Hittite form, in the second millennium, has five separate parts. It begins with a *preface* in which the king identifies himself, "I am the great king." Then he mentions in an *historical prologue* all that he had done and what an all-around, wonderful fellow he is. Having established this greatness, the relationship between himself (the great gift to society) and the world, as the one who saves all the vassal kings, particularly the one to whom he is writing at the moment. Then he goes on to set up his *stipulations*. "In view of all this," he writes, "I would like you to do the following." Then he closes the treaty with the reminder that he has *blessings and curses* from all the gods that he can think of, both in his own country and the other fellow's country. He wants to make sure that none are left out, and that no god is going to leap from the bushes and bring a hex on him. The treaty finally concludes by mentioning the *provision for royal succession*. Now here, Meredith Kline says in effect, "Eureka, we have just found the outline [the literary form and outline] for the book of Deuteronomy."

And that's precisely how it goes. Deuteronomy 1:1-5 is the preface. Chapter 1:6 through chapter 4 is the historical prologue, in which God "the great King" reviews His vassal treaty or His covenant with the people of Israel. Then from the beginning of chapter 5 through chapter 26, there are the stipulations or laws, of

---

5. Meredith Kline, *The Treaty of the Great King* (Grand Rapids: Eerdmans Publishing Co., 1963). See also Kenneth A. Kitchen, *The Ancient Orient and the Old Testament* (Chicago: Inter-Varsity Press, 1966), pp. 90-102.

God, followed by chapters 27–30 with its blessings and curses, which were to be given on Mount Ebal and Mount Gerizim. Finally, in chapters 31–34, there are provisions for succession. And Kline suggests: "Don't you see that if you say the text must have been *written* in the first millennium, after a long oral tradition of many accurate details, then you would have two of these parts left out, as in the treaties of Esarhaddon and Aramaic treaties? But the literary form which was in vogue, was one which must be written back in 1500 to 1400 B.C., which is precisely the time when we've been saying that Moses wrote the Pentateuch!"

Not only has archaeology demonstrated that the things in the Books of Moses are true, but now Kline dares to say that *as it is written,* it belongs back in that period. The literary genre says that it must belong there in the second millennium B.C. And that is the most brilliant demonstration that I have ever seen. I maintain that it is so good that no one has yet given a reply to Kline's book and his conclusions. And I think that in itself is a very, very eloquent comment. So much for Kline's great book, *Treaty of the Great King.*

This then is the historian working on the past. In addition to the foregoing, though, let us look at the theology of the Historical Books themselves. Here I would like briefly to take up, as an example, the Book of Chronicles. This book is probably the most theological of all of the Historical Books.

I dare you to make a real study of the Book of Chronicles. Use it for your own quiet time, your devotions. Perhaps you have tried and cannot get past chapters 1 to 9: "So and so begat, so and so begat!" Well, begin at chapter 10 then, though there is a valid use for all the material in chapters 1 to 9. Perhaps we can consider that later. But for now, note that the Book of Chronicles itself is a beautiful collection of theological concepts.

For example, Chronicles is a book of revivals. Read II Chronicles 15, the story of Asa; or the account of the deliverance under Jehoshaphat, in chapter 20. Or in chapters 23–24, read about the revival by Jehoiada under Joash, and in chapters 29–31, the revival under Hezekiah; and in chapter 25, under Amaziah. There are at least five different revivals that are explicitly noted in these passages.

As a matter of fact, that's one of the important aspects of this book. Perhaps the most familiar verse in regard to revival is in II Chronicles 7:14: "If My people, which are called by my name, shall humble themselves, and pray, and seek my face, and turn from their wicked ways; then will I hear from heaven, and will forgive their sin, and will heal their land." But there are sixty-four more chapters in the two Books of Chronicles in which the writer is looking back over the history of Israel, and he dares to put a theological interpretation and its stamp and flavor upon it.

Out of the full sixty-five chapters, nineteen of them are devoted to David. First Chronicles 11–29 includes the account of David, who is the most important man by all odds in the book. But this is not mere idol or hero worship. David is the man who is presented in such an important way because he represents the Messiah who is to come, as can also be seen in another historical record, II Samuel 7.

All that God has planned to do in history, and in the ages to come, is wrapped up in this man David and in his particular genealogy. That is why Saul gets one chapter (I Chron. 10), which is a theological chapter at that. Clearly, Saul is not the man through whom God will work. There is the comment in I Samuel 31 that Saul, at the battle of Gilboa, took his sword out and fell upon it. He saw that his end was near, and he helped it along. This same event is repeated in I Chronicles 10:4, with this addition in verse 14, that "the Lord . . . slew him."

Compare the materials that are synoptically placed in the Books of Samuel and Kings. It is an excellent study in human responsibility and divine sovereignty. Whereas the Books of Samuel and Kings will usually stress the former, Chronicles will assert that the divine hand is at work. The identical events that are recorded in Chronicles are viewed from a theological perspective. These same acts are attributed to God. (Notice these passages: I Chron. 11:9; 21:7; II Chron. 10:15; 11:4; 12:2; 13:18; 14:11-12; 17-3; 5; 18:31; 20:30; 21:10; 22:7, 25:20.)

Let me illustrate further. In I Chronicles 10 it says the Lord slew Saul. He did? Yes, He did. Because under His control Saul had ruled. Then he had come to the end of his strength. Saul didn't know that he had been given a gift, but it was by the gift of the Holy Spirit that he ruled at all. In his earlier life, Saul was naturally a retiring sort of fellow. When they looked for a leader, he was in hiding. He didn't seem like a natural leader at all. Perhaps in a college today, his class could have voted him the most unlikely to succeed, except perhaps in basketball or football. He was head and shoulders, physically, above his fellows.

Yet, on the other hand, when the Spirit of God came upon him, Saul came forth and all of a sudden he had a personality change. He sacrificed his oxen, sent them out in twelve parts, calling on the twelve tribes to follow him. He got them to believe that they could go up to the other side of Jordan and release those prisoners in Jabesh-Gilead. There was a big job to do. Saul was able to do it, because the Spirit of God came upon him.

After he had three times transgressed the specific command of God, however, God took His hand off him, and the Spirit of God left him. His ability to rule and to lead were gone; he was unable to perform any longer and was completely incompetent. The end was swift, as it will be for all who in self-will forget God.

Well, that's Saul. But there are other chapters where the same dilemma of sovereignty and freedom takes place. It is found in the account of Jehosophat's ships in the harbor at Elath. In I Kings 22:47 it says that a storm came up and destroyed them. In II Chronicles 20:37 it says that God destroyed the ships. Each one of these accounts is very instructive, particularly if someone gets embroiled in the Arminian/Calvinistic debate! When the accounts are put together, rather than conflicting with each other they come off rather as "Calvominian," since the writer tries to show that there is the sovereignty of God—that there is a place in which God Himself ultimately is in control of all these things, but also that men are responsible, too.

Reading these passages together becomes tremendously instructive, with both of these concepts functioning.

Then the Book of Chronicles also deals with the "heart." There are at least thirty references made about the heart, which is referred to as the right and necessary relationship with God. God requires a perfect heart, and those thirty references talk about the necessity of a right heart condition.

As one example, there is the famous text of II Chronicles 16:9, "For the eyes of the Lord run to and fro throughout the whole earth, to show himself strong in behalf of them whose heart is perfect toward him." Azariah the prophet had said to Asa in II Chronicles 15:2, ". . . The Lord is with you, while ye be with him; and if ye seek him, he will be found of you; but if ye forsake him, He will forsake you." Seeking the Lord with one's total inner man, one's heart, is the essence of true Biblical faith.

There are many other themes, but let me just list them without seeking a full definition of them. The Bible student can dig them out for himself.

Chronicles is also a book of prayer. Did you know there are eighty-five complete prayers in the Old Testament? And in reading them, we see that God not only changes men, but He changes things, too. I know that's not a Bible verse; it's a motto. But the motto reflects Biblical theology. And it's true. The efficacy of prayer is dealt with in Chronicles. We note the universalism of God—as He brings up the Syrians, as He moves the Assyrians, and as He uses the Babylonians. It is God who says to them, "I have a job for you to do." It is the Lord Himself who directs them. It is God who puts down those nations, too, who think in their pride that they did all these great exploits in their own power. God is the One wielding the axe, even when it is used against Israel. But the nations must not think that they are wielding the axe themselves, or God will show them differently (Isa. 10:15).

Chronicles also has a strong emphasis on the importance of worship. Chronicles is a book of worship, with the center in Jerusalem. But it is not concerned just with the mechanics of worship, but also with true worship of the living God Himself.

Let us close this section with that beautiful passage in I Chronicles 29, where David thanked God for all the offerings that were given. He mentioned how the people offered themselves willingly, and then he prayed this prayer, found in I Chronicles 29:10-14:

> Wherefore David blessed the Lord before all the congregation: and David said, Blessed be thou, Lord God of Israel our father, for ever and ever. Thine, O Lord, is the greatness and the power, and the glory, and the victory, and the majesty: for all that is in the heaven and in the earth is thine; thine is the kingdom, O Lord, and thou art exalted as head above all. Both riches and honour come of thee, and thou reignest over all: and in thine hand is power and might; and in thine hand it is to make great, and to give strength unto all. Now therefore, our God, we thank thee, and praise thy glorious name. But who am I, and what is my people, that we should be able

> to offer so willingly after this sort? For all things come
> of thee, and of thine own have we given thee.

The people had offered everything for the building of the temple, so David said to the Lord, "Lord, these things belong to You in the first place. We're just giving back to You what You have given to us. And it's so marvelous that You've worked upon the hearts of Your men. This is a beautiful thing in our eyes." Then David, the man after God's own heart, goes on to describe God in terms that are only rivaled by that mighty passage of Isaiah 40.

This historian's view of the past, the present, and the future, is a beautiful thing to behold. Our Lord shows us true history, "His Story," and brings it alive for our day or for any day, and for our instruction.

# The Witness of the Prophets

## Proclaiming the Promise

The Old Testament prophets were men of varied ages, characters, and idiosyncrasies. Even today they are viewed in various ways. Were they revolutionaries or were they conservatives? Today they are being considered, particularly by young people, and especially in the university setting, as justification for both theoretical and actual revolution.

The prophets, so we are told, were old-time revolutionaries. Perhaps there is some truth to the statement. But I would like to qualify that term "revolutionary." Many people in using the phrase "liberty, equality, and fraternity" have turned to the prophets and have sought inspiration from them. There is a vast difference, however, between our contemporary concept of a revolutionary and the actual practice of those prophets themselves.

They were men of words: so are our present-day revolutionaries. Many students today stand on the steps of many a university and pour out their words in an unending, and often unintelligible, stream. Of course, the contrast to us is very obvious. The prophets were men of *God's Word*, a vast difference from *man's word*. They wrote, "Thus saith the Lord," about fifty-three hundred times; thus over and over again in the Old Testament, there is this key reference. Today's would-be prophets repeat, "I say," "I feel," and "I think that. . . ."

There is another contrast. The revolutionaries of today appeal to the masses. They appeal to them to rise up against tyranny, against the "unjust establishment," against the social order that has gone awry. And in many cases the appeal is justified. The establishment has, in many instances, really turned on itself. Later on you will see why I say that, but for different reasons than many are using today.

But the prophets of old did not appeal to the crowds. They did not appeal to the masses. They did call for revolution—but here comes the great contrast. They appealed basically to the individual. They wanted something to happen to the individual first. They did not appeal to the institution. They did not appeal to society in general. They longed for something radical to happen inside of the individual person. Then, perhaps, the institutions and society might be affected. Certainly this is the tenor of the gospel message.

As a matter of fact, if we could only understand it, that's precisely the mandate God has given to us, as we appeal to men. The first word of all our appeals, in the Name of Jesus Christ, should be for the individual to repent; to repent and turn again. Repentance is the key word in the prophets. It is where they always begin.

These men of old were basically two things. They were *forthtellers* as well as *foretellers*. We always seem to put the foretelling ahead of the forth-telling. We think of them as predictors, trying to pre-write history rather than understanding that they were also, and more importantly, forth-tellers, preachers of God's Word. As a matter of fact, they did foretell the future, but only that men might be moved to repent while in their present situation.

Prophecy in the Bible, and all discussion of the future, is not there only for our curiosity or for our special charts. We are not supposed to be making grandiloquent kinds of statements about what God can do in the future. Incidentally, whenever we find a prediction, an eschatological event, which is referred to in either Testament, we surely find in that same context that it includes a great lever, a wedge, which is also used to move us *now* toward godly, holy living.

Seeing then that these things shall come to pass; seeing that this is the kind of God who is going to act in the future; seeing that this is one aspect of His plan for the future, what sort of men ought we to be here and now, today? A holy urgency will come upon us to be a holy people, that we be men and women who are forgiven, able to "look God in the eye," and hence able to look each other in the eye. That is what is meant in the I John 1:7 passage, where it says that if we are walking "in the light, as he is in the light, we have fellowship one with another, and the blood of Jesus Christ his Son cleanseth us from all sin." And this is all taking place because men are responding to the basic prophetic call to repentance.

Personal repentance, then, is the key to corporate societal change. How does one change a nation? The world? How do we change society? They are changed by the first and most radical way of all, through the hearts of individual men and women. Change the heart of one individual, or a nation, and you'll change everything from the sociological to the political structure. Everything else will be sure to follow.

As a matter of fact, this has ever been the human experience. Education stands in dire need of regeneration. But does it need a new program, a new philosophy, more buildings? It does not! Education is currently crumbling. Buildings and equipment can be, and are being, destroyed. Programs and philosophies can be, and are being, rejected. What is needed is some substance—a revival, a change, in the hearts of men. It is startling and revealing to realize that a very high percentage of the institutions of higher learning in North America were started as a result of a spiritual awakening, of revival fires that spread through the land.

Go back through the history of most of these institutions, before the land grant colleges, and we find that they are the result of a response to a tremendous outpouring of the Spirit of God.

To see education move forward in Canada or the States, pray God that there will come another revival. But not only a revival, a reformation as well; for we must look for the two of them simultaneously. It is not just that people might come to know Christ, that they might have an initial experience with Him. They must also be discipled (cf. Matt. 28:18-20). And in the discipling of men and women there is the study of the Scriptures. It is essential that the hunger of people for the Word of God be satisfied. The "disciples" must get involved in the study of the Bible. Then, and only then, will we see a genuine reformation.

Revival speaks of a regeneration of life. Reformation speaks of a return to that Biblical Word, and living according to it, as a real substance. It will be reformation that will conserve the real fruits of revival when it comes. The two of them must always be together.

Reformation alone leads to the disease of "intellectualism." Revival alone can lead to a subjectivism devoid of a point of reference. But the subjective and the objective side by side—this is what the prophets declared was essential for mankind.

Let me illustrate this from Jeremiah 7. Here is a stormy message, given by this prophet of the Lord, which points up both the forthteller aspect and the emphasis that he placed on repentance. He was terribly upset with the structures of his time. He said, almost in the language of today, that the institutions of society were shot through with wickedness. They were finished unless there would be repentance.

Is the proper response to prop up the institution or to tear it down? Both of them are false. One can become a hyper-loyalist to the institution, and say that whether right or wrong it must be conserved. That doesn't seem Biblically correct. Others say, "The institution is rotten, let's pull it down." But that's not the right way either, because when it is down, there are still the people who are left behind. And then suddenly it dawns on us that perhaps the people are the ones who are the trouble, and not the buildings or the organizations! We thought that the problem was the institution. Long ago, my grandfather said half jokingly, "If only it weren't for men and women, churches would be real fine." Perhaps he had a point, because it is the men and women who are the real problems in the world.

In many ways, this is a delightful sermon in Jeremiah 7. But it is an awesome message as well. The prophet stood outside the entrance to the temple preaching. The people were going in to worship, and Jeremiah preached at them! Can you imagine standing outside one of the local churches today, and preaching a sermon against the people who think they are going in to get another sermon?

But Jeremiah stood there, and in verses 2 and 3 we read, ". . . Hear the word of the Lord, all ye of Judah, that enter in at these gates to worship the Lord. Thus saith the Lord of Hosts, the God of Israel, Amend your ways and your doings, and I will cause you to dwell in this place."

Can you imagine the people nudging each other as they go in, saying, "Who's this fellow? What's he trying to tell us? That we might live in another place than this one? Does he know something we don't know?"

The point of the whole matter is, Jeremiah did know something they didn't know. They didn't know what was going to happen to them if they didn't repent. So Jeremiah called on them to "amend their ways and their doings." That's not just tautology or filling up the Bible with repetitive or useless words. This phrase refers to the tilt of a man's life, the direction in which he is going, and his actual deeds. They both fall under the judgment of God. Some people don't do evil, perhaps, but they lean awfully far in that general direction! They have a mental or spiritual tilt that leans that way. The Bible speaks both of a man's bias and of his actual deeds. God says man must repent of both of them, bring them both into line with His divine will and purpose.

Do you ever find yourself leaning more and more in the direction that opposes God's dictum for your life? The Bible says to amend it, to repent of it. It calls for personal repentance. Then why didn't Israel do it? What was the problem? The people were too "establishment" centered. Jeremiah 7:4 says, "Trust ye not in lying words, saying, The temple of the Lord, The temple of the Lord, The temple of the Lord, are these." That's almost a chant. But the people were so hard of hearing, so hard of heart, that it had to be repeated over and over until they believed it.

Perhaps they heard it, but they got used to it and said, as perhaps even we do: "That will never happen here!"

Think of all the wonderful things we have. Start naming off the churches, the Bible colleges, and all the strong Christian institutions of today. Aren't these impressive to the Lord? Look what He would miss! Perhaps the people of Jeremiah's day said the same thing about Jerusalem. If he destroys Jerusalem, where will His holy name go? Where will He have a place of residence? He already had said that Jerusalem and the temple were to be His place of residence. It will never happen here!

Today, some people might say that in the Chicago area, too— that center of evangelicalism, where there are so many fine Christian organizations—that judgment couldn't come to Chicago! Where would God go? What would He do for a center for evangelicalism? Think how many mission societies have their headquarters in Wheaton and Chicago. No, it couldn't happen there at all. In effect, what is being said is: "The temple of the Lord . . . The temple of the Lord, are these." Nothing can disturb it.

But Jeremiah said:

> If ye thoroughly amend your ways and your doings; if ye thoroughly execute judgment between a man and his neighbour; if ye oppress not the stranger, the fatherless, and the widow, and shed not innocent blood in this place, neither walk after other gods to your hurt, then

will I cause you to dwell in this place, in the land that I gave to your fathers, for ever and ever. Behold, ye trust in lying words, that cannot profit. Will ye steal, murder, and commit adultery, and swear falsely, and burn incense unto Baal . . . (Jer. 7:5-9)?

The prophets were preachers of the commandments and they were preachers of the Law. Jeremiah preached the Law back to them. Why? Notice his words: ". . . and walk not after other gods whom ye know not; and come and stand before me in this house, which is called by my name, and say, We are delivered to do all these abominations" (Jer. 7:9-10). They really didn't speak like that, but they *lived* like that. They lived vile lives on the outside and then said, "Now let us go to the house of the Lord," and they walked to the temple. They went in to worship a holy God.

Then Jeremiah thundered at them: "If in going to God's house you go there with no intent to confess your sins, to repent, to change, then you are making God's house a place for robbers and thieves. It's not only that you *have* sins, but that you *keep* your sins. You go in there and pretend that the Lord doesn't know all about it, and that it's all swept under the rug. You think, 'let's forget about it.' So you walk out of the temple, having paid the required outward respects to God, saying 'See, we are delivered. We are the people of God.' " What a travesty of religion and worship.

In one of my classes I have a Hebrew Christian who is quite a wit. One day he jokingly asserted, "You can't touch me." Curiously I asked, "Why not?" His response: "I'm one of the Chosen People!" Perhaps those people of Jeremiah's day had the same concept, too. For the prophet said in verse 11, "Is this house, which is called by my name, become a den of robbers in your eyes? Behold, even I have seen it, saith the Lord."

And what did He advise them to do? In verse 12 He said, "You say that it can never happen in Jerusalem. Why don't you go over to Shiloh and kick the ashes around. Just think of where the tabernacle stood at one time. Remember? Didn't I bring the tabernacle from the wilderness? Where did I put it? I put it in Shiloh. Look there. See where My name used to be. How does it look now? Empty. Desolate. And now you're telling Me it can never happen here in Jerusalem? Remember Shiloh." This is the motive for Jeremiah's message. And he told the people to remember and repent.

Here is a tremendous message so badly needed today. Are we afraid to preach it? Are we so feeble and frightened that we can stand before the Living God and still not tell men and women that they are really headed for destruction? We are really playing with fire, for "our God is a consuming fire." North American society is headed for destruction and judgment. And we had better believe it's coming, because there is no sign that repentance is near. It is coming, or else God is a liar and His word is not true. The prophet's message must be preached again today.

The world is seeking a change, and sometimes the Christian segment is less aware of this than is the non-Christian segment. The non-Christian world is groaning within itself and exposing the complete inadequacy of what it knows. They have tried everything. Some of the younger men and women have copped out of society completely. They say that there is nothing—no answer, no meaning to life. Then some of them find Jesus Christ.

To really understand the prophets, one must see them in these terms. This is the great discovery in the books of the prophets. They were real men who were trying to bring real people back to a real God. This is the true meaning of the call to repent. It means that although we were heading off in one direction—toward our own plans, now God says, "Turn. Accept My plan and My program." That's the whole thrust of this passage in Jeremiah 7—God seeking to turn men back to Himself.

There is a second emphasis that is found in the Prophets. There is not only repentance, but there is also a heavy stress upon some of the more important things in the Law. The prophets were preachers of the Law. Read Jeremiah 7:21-23. But in preaching the Law, Jeremiah saw that there are some things in the Law that are more important than other aspects of the Law. I must affirm that the Law is one. But there are some things that are more important than others within the Law.

Someone might ask me, "How do you know that this is so?" My reply would be that Jesus talked about it in Matthew 23:23, where we read, "Woe unto you, scribes and Pharisees, hypocrites! for ye pay tithe of mint and anise and cummin, and have omitted *the weightier matters* of the law" (italics mine). And what are the weightier matters of the Law? Because if words have any meaning,

Jesus said some things are heavier, some things are more important than others. Some things have higher rank within the Law. And when He tells us that there are some things that are heavier—some things that are weightier—we must pause until we understand it, since He went on to say: ". . . judgment, mercy and faith: these ought ye to have done, and not to leave the other undone." This is our Lord's teaching. And from where did He get those words? From another prophet. Read Micah 6:6-8.

Pursuing this further, in Matthew 12:7, we see the same thing. There was a discussion about the Sabbath day and about Sabbath observance. Our Lord was trying to help the Pharisees who were criticizing His disciples because they ate some grain as they were going through the field.

Jesus again referred to the Prophets, this time to Hosea 6:6, to teach the weightier aspects of the Law. He also used the passage about David, saying, "Haven't you read what David did?" And what does David have to do with eating some grain on the Sabbath, especially since they were hungry? The point is: There was a command in the ceremonial Law, which said you shouldn't eat the shewbread. But David and his men were hungry, and therefore they gave David what was not lawful to give. In other words, the Law was there, but there was an understood, suppressed *ceteris paribus,* "all other things being equal," idea. So David was given the shewbread even though the Old Testament Law said, "Don't eat the shewbread."

Here was an exception that proved the rule, our Lord said. So He argued the same way with regard to the Sabbath day.

Read on to Matthew 12:6: "But I say unto you, That in this place is one greater than the temple. But if ye had known what this meaneth, I will have mercy, and not sacrifice, ye would not have condemned the guiltless." In other words, Jesus was saying that you shouldn't be so 'hung up' on your question about the ceremonial aspect of the Law. If you would only understand what Hosea 6:6 is saying—if you would only get that part clear—you wouldn't have this problem. Why don't you think on that? Why don't you go home and learn what that means, 'I will have mercy and not sacrifice.' Did I ask for sacrifice? Did I write the Book of Leviticus, with all the sacrificial ordinances?" And we reply, "You did!" Well then, why does He now say He doesn't want it? Why does He say He'll have mercy without sacrifice?

Let us search a little further. In Matthew 9, we read of another appeal to Micah 6:6. There the Pharisees observe that Jesus is eating in the house of tax collectors and sinners. They question such socializing by saying, "Why is your Master eating with publicans and sinners?" Then in verse 12, Jesus replies by saying, "They that be whole need not a physician, but they that are sick."

I've often used this passage when people say that all the sinners are in the church. Often outsiders mention a certain deacon or the skeletons of past scandals of the church as excuses for not coming themselves. Then I tell them, "Well you know that's the truth. Bad people go to church, good people go to the golf course. Jesus said so. They that are sick go to the hospital. Bad people go to church."

There is one big difference. They know that they're bad. The sad thing is, they should get some help from the Good Book while they're there. But too often, the so-called good, or well, people go to church, but they don't get into the emergency ward at all. They just stand around on the fringes or in the vestibule and watch the people coming in and going out. Also, it's a sad commentary on Christian profession, when the ones who look down on the sick, the needy, and the sinful, don't get down and help them.

So if there are a lot of sinners in church, that's what church is all about. That's why I go to church.

In Matthew 9:13 Jesus says, "But go ye and learn what that meaneth, I will have mercy, and not sacrifice: for I am not come to call the righteous, but sinners to repentance." Why not learn what Hosea 6:6 means? What is our Lord talking about? It is the same message that Jeremiah 7:21-23 has for us. Doubtless, there are Christian people who have read that verse, but they have thought for sure that their Bible had a misprint in it.

Sometimes I test my classes by having someone read aloud Jeremiah 7:21-23 for the class. He reads through the text quickly: "Put your burnt offerings unto your sacrifices, and eat flesh, for I spake not unto your fathers. . . ." I stop them there, and say, "Excuse me, you misread the passage. Shouldn't it read, 'For I *spake* unto your fathers and commanded them in the day that I brought them out of the land of Egypt, concerning burnt offerings or sacrifices'?" "Oh, no," the reader says, "my Bible reads 'not.' " Then I say, "What do you have? Some poor translation?" I know what he's reading, but I'm playing with him, you see. I want to call the attention of the class to verse 22, where it says: "For I spake *not* unto your fathers, nor commanded them in the day that I brought them out of the land of Egypt, concerning burnt offerings or sacrifices."

Then someone with a good background of Old Testament says, "That's not true; He did command sacrifices." I reply, "He did?" The student asserts, "We know He did, Leviticus records it."

Now the modernist gets hold of this passage and says, "See, we told you Leviticus was of a later date. We knew it wasn't written in that early period. It was a later inscription. The Bible itself says so! There's the proof." Then the modernist become a literalist on this one verse only, just at that point. They believe one word. They hold their finger on the word, "not, not, not." They keep pointing to it. There are one or two verses they really believe, and this is one of them. Too bad they don't believe more words or verses! And they don't see what the author's meaning is, even in that verse under discussion.

Jeremiah 7:23 goes on to say, "But this thing commanded I them, saying, Obey my voice, and I will be your God, and ye shall be my people; and walk ye in all the ways that I have commanded you. . . ." How did this enter in? Have we seen it before? What did Jeremiah say? He declared that God said something like this: "I did not speak to you, nor command you in the day that I brought you out of the land of Egypt, for the sake of burnt offerings and sacrifices. I wasn't interested in being fed. If I were hungry [and this is also found in Psalm 50], I wouldn't need to come to you and say, could you spare a bull or an ox, or could you give me a sheep? I own the cattle on a thousand hills, they are all Mine. You don't need to feed Me. That's not the import of the sacrifice. I don't need them. That wasn't why I spoke to you. Don't you understand why I spoke to you, why I said this to you, 'Obey My voice, and I will be your God'?"

Incidentally, that phrase "I will be your God" is from Genesis; "And you shall be My people"—that's from Exodus; "And walk ye in all the ways that I have commanded you"—that's from Deuteronomy. God is repeating His promise theme again and thereby urging Israel to participate in these everlasting benefits.

Our paraphrase goes on, "That's what I said to you. I wanted you to respond with your whole heart." The point to note is simply this: God inspects the man first, and then He inspects his offering. We find this in both the Old and New Testaments.

In Genesis 4 we have the record of the sacrifices of Cain and Abel. Do you know what the significance of that account is? Note the text. It says that Cain and Abel brought their offerings. It was time to show for worship—so Cain brought his offering, and Abel brought his offering.

But Abel brought of the fat pieces, the firstlings of his flock. "And the Lord *had respect* unto Abel and to his offering." Did you ever notice that and wonder why the Bible uses the verb, "He had respect"? You don't *have respect* unto offerings, you *accept* them. We use that verb "respect" for people. But God "had respect unto Abel." Then it says, "and to his offering." Don't you see the text says that God looked at the man first, and then He looked at his offering?

"But unto Cain and to his offering," God did "not have respect." Why? Because God investigated the heart. What was the difference between the two offerings? I know what comes to your mind. But the text says that the word that's used for offering is actually "a gift." It's the same one that's used in Leviticus 2 for a "meal offering." So both men are bringing "gift offerings" to God. So if both of them brought gifts, why was there such a difference in God's response? What was the real contrast? It was in the hearts of the men.

Perhaps you say, but I know some New Testament references that you've forgotten about. For instance, in Hebrews 11: "By faith Abel offered." That's the point. Abel offered a more excellent sacrifice because he offered it in faith, out of a total commitment of himself to God. It was not done as routine. It wasn't because it was the proper time to worship; it wasn't formalistic; it wasn't ritualistic; and it wasn't because he had to do it. It was an expression of the inside, of the man himself.

On the same topic, many think we refer to the text that mentions the "blood of Abel" and prove that this is the real difference in the offerings. That reference is found in Hebrews 12:24, where we read more fully that the blood of Christ speaks better things than the blood of Abel. The blood of Christ pleads mercy for us. The blood of Abel, mentioned in that text, is his own blood that was spilt on the ground by Cain. It cries out and pleads, "Somebody, help." It pleads for vengeance. But the blood of Christ pleads for mercy. You will see that this is the point in this particular text. The same type of reference may be found in I John 1:7 and Jude 21.

The sacrifices mentioned in the Old Testament, and particularly as announced by the prophets, are deeds in which God was primarily looking at the internal preparation of the man's heart. Then He began looking at the external preparation of the man's heart. Then He began looking at the external signs and forms as they expressed the theology of a ransom by a substitute who was to come.

Let me illustrate this truth as it is found elsewhere in the Old Testament. In Isaiah 1:11-18, the prophet announced to the people,

> To what purpose is the multitude of your sacrifices unto me? saith the Lord: I am full ["I'm sick and tired," we would say] of the burnt offerings of rams, and the fat of fed beasts; and I delight not in the blood of bullocks, or of lambs, or of he goats. When ye come to appear before me, who hath required this at your hand, to tread my courts? Bring no more vain oblations; incense is an abomination unto me; the new moons and sabbaths, the calling of assemblies, I cannot away with; it is iniquity, even the solemn meeting. Your new moons and your appointed feasts my soul hateth; they are a trouble unto me; I am weary to bear them. And when ye spread forth your hands, I will hide mine eyes from you. . . .

That verse has deeply impressed me. We spread out our hands, and say "Now let us pray." Not that God has eyes or that He has to hide them. But He says in effect, "I'm not going to even regard your prayer; go ahead and do your little thing, and let Me know when it's all over. I don't want anything from you, I'll have no part of it at all." As the text continues,

> I will hide mine eyes from you: yea, when you make many prayers, I will not hear: your hands are full of blood. Wash you, make you clean; put away the evil of your doings from before mine eyes; cease to do evil; learn to do well; seek judgment, relieve the oppressed,

judge the fatherless, plead for the widow. Come now, and let us reason together, saith the Lord: though your sins be as scarlet, they shall be as white as snow; though they be red like crimson, they shall be as wool.

Did God speak to the men regarding sacrifices only? Is that all God was concerned with? No, never in a thousand years. What was the more important thing? The hearts of the men. If the hearts of the men were not prepared to sacrifice, it might just as well have been left undone. Save the goat. Otherwise it's a wasted sacrifice —good for neither God, the sacrificer, nor the goat.

There are many other passages that deal with the same theme. One is in Hosea 6, just one of several that Jesus quoted. Notice the words. In themselves they provide a beautiful sermon, even as they present profound truth. Notice particularly Hosea 6:4 ff: "O Ephraim, what shall I do unto thee? O Judah, what shall I do unto thee? For your goodness is as a morning cloud, and as the early dew it goeth away." Isn't that beautiful? Well, isn't God also working today? Don't we hear of revival and salvation across these lands?

Yes, but as Hosea says, it's like the morning dew. Put a little heat on it, and puff, it's gone. It just isn't there any more. Goodness was there, but it evaporated. There was nothing to sustain it.

Then Hosea says, "Therefore have I hewed them by the prophets." God lays them low with the prophets, using His Word, "by the words of my mouth." To make a play on words, God slays them with His word so that they won't be slain by the sword! If we only knew how to use words, particularly His Word! Words often cut, but they're a lot nicer; and the wounds from words heal a lot quicker than those wounds inflicted by the enemy's sword. Which would you rather have? God says, "Therefore have I hewed them by the prophets; I have slain them by the words of my mouth: and thy judgments are as the light that goeth forth. For I desired mercy and not sacrifice; and the knowledge of God more than burnt offerings."

This is the precise passage that our Lord Jesus Christ quoted. Let us think seriously about this. Do we think we know the Bible? We don't know the Bible until we can understand this. We don't know the Old Testament until we understand this.

Don't just say that I understand back in the Old Testament they used to bring sacrifices because they had to do it. It's far more than that. Listen to what the Lord said here: "I desired mercy more than sacrifice."

Turn to the Book of Micah 6:6-8. This prophet asks a rhetorical question: "Wherewith shall I come before the Lord, and bow myself before the high God? shall I come before him with burnt offerings, with calves of a year old? Will the Lord be pleased with thousands of rams, or with ten thousands of rivers of oil? shall I give my firstborn for my transgression, the fruit of my body for the sin of my soul?"

Notice the sweep of his question. It was all right when he asked about rams, even thousands of them, or about ten thousand rivers of oil. These are astronomical figures, but even then we could think in those terms. But then to introduce that other practice—something pagan at that—a human sacrifice of the oldest son. This is too much. The man was really desperate. What does God want from me, he cries? What does He want? What shall I give Him. How can I really get this load of sin off my back? How can there be "at-one-ment" between God and myself?

Then the answer comes in Micah 6:8. "He has showed thee, O man, what is good; and what doth the Lord require of thee, but to do justly, to love mercy, and to walk humbly with thy God." Once again the modernist has picked this up, and has said, "Ah. This is just a Boy Scout slogan. Help an old lady across the street today—do your good deed. And God will smile upon you."

Personally I think that is not too bad. We should be helpful and kind. But the point is they have misunderstood the real intent of the passage if that's all it says to them. Jesus quoted this very verse in Matthew 23:23 when He said, "Ye . . . have omitted the weightier matters of the law, judgment [or justice], mercy, and faith." He translated "walking humbly with thy God" as "faith." That was Jesus' commentary, pointing out that there are some weightier matters in the Law. If only we could understand that there are some things that are heavier. Here's one of them. This is heavier. This ranks as number one. And we cannot understand the Bible, we cannot understand the Old Testament, until we understand how this ranks as number one with God.

There are many verses similar to this.

Perhaps you recall a Sunday school lesson of years ago. It was on Samuel and Saul, as told in I Samuel 15. Saul thought that if only he could bring back a big offering to the Lord, that would be acceptable; perhaps raise his stock with God a few points. He thought it would be a shame just to kill all the animals taken in battle without getting any sacrificial mileage out of them, just because the Lord said so. He must have thought he could get some spiritual benefit or leverage from them. He would bring all those cattle back and present a huge sacrifice to the Lord.

Did he really think this would get him in good with the Lord? Most likely. But Samuel came along and said to him, "What's all this that I hear? The bleating of the sheep, and the lowing of the cattle?"

"Oh," says Saul, "I'm glad you asked! We brought a sacrifice for the Lord. I know you'll be pleased."

To which Samuel retorted, "Pleased? Does the Lord have as great a delight in sacrifice as He has in obedience? Behold, to obey is better than to sacrifice, and to hearken than the fat of rams." And here I think Saul was crushed because he didn't know his Bible. He didn't understand God. He thought that sacrifices were all that was needed. As long as they were given, credit was received. But no, God looks at the man, at the heart first of all. Obedience is number one in our priorities of serving Him. Sacrifice follows.

Let me cite just once more experience that carries out this theme. It's found in Psalm 51. Here is one of the most beautiful examples of what kind of sins can be forgiven. I was taught to understand that only unwitting sins could be forgiven in the Old Testament era. I was taught that on the basis of Numbers 15. But while there is a distinction between witting and unwitting sins, I also found out that in Leviticus and in Numbers there were a good many sins that could be confessed to the Lord, for which there was full and free forgiveness.

I should have known better, because Psalm 32 and Psalm 51 remind us that an adulterer or even a murderer can find forgiveness with God. These were precisely David's sins.

In Psalm 32, David tells the story of how he was on the outs with God for almost a full year, until that child of his sin was born. For those nine months he went through the throes of agony and remorse. He uses desperate figures of speech to depict his condition: his bones almost dried up; his moisture was like summertime; he was like a desert. His experience with God—this man after God's own heart—was sheer agony for that gestation period. He never wanted to experience anything like it again. Take those days away, he pled.

And as he finally came to the end of himself, he said, "O God, I confess my sins." And God forgave him! "And thou, God forgavest me." That is what the text says. Sin is forgiven and sin is forgotten.

God didn't say, "David, don't you dare be king anymore. Don't you dare lead My people anymore." No! His sins were forgiven, and his sins were forgotten. That's the message we hold out to modern man. There are many men who would give anything if they could go to sleep at night. They can. There's good news for them. Once my four-year-old boy came home from Sunday school at Christmastime. I said, "What was the story about?" He said, "Angel said, 'got good news.'" That's the message of the whole Bible—"got good news!"

The good news also is found in Psalm 51, where David reflects on that earlier experience. He said in verse 16: "For thou desirest not sacrifice; else would I give it: thou delightest not in burnt offering. The sacrifices of God are a broken spirit: a broken and a contrite heart, O God, thou wilt not despise." Then he goes on to say in verse 19, "Then shalt thou be pleased with the sacrifices of righteousness. . . ." Do you see that? A broken heart first, and then the note of assurance that God will "be pleased with the sacrifices. . . ."

The prophets were preachers of the Law, and in preaching the Law they said that there were weightier matters, things that must be understood first. It was this whole matter of a person's internal relationship—whether or not his heart was right with God; whether or not he had repented first. Then God could inspect both his offering and his worship. He could then inspect his tithe and everything else that he brought.

Doesn't that open up the Old Testament for you? Do you see how it's really the same today as it was then? We are the same type of people. He is the same God!

Nevertheless, although the prophets were primarily forthtellers, they were also foretellers, or predictors. They were talking of events that were to come. And these events were given so that the people of that day might "shape up"—that the knowledge of them might be a motivating force in their lives.

Did you know that I Corinthians 15, the resurrection chapter which I love so much, contains quotations from the Old Testament? In that chapter, if I might paraphrase it loosely, we read: "Come on, death, give it all you have. Do your worst, I dare you. O grave, come on, show us what you can do." Here Paul deliberately dares to taunt death. Death is the archenemy of each of us. I hate it with a consuming passion. I've stood at the graveside of many a person—and some of my own loved ones—and I hate what death means.

Our Lord says it's His enemy. He says it's the last enemy that He's going to get. And I know He will get it but good. He will do it in. I hate death with a passion. And I know you do, too.

But having given that whole thrust there, Paul goes on and ends up triumphantly in that fifteenth chapter with these magnificent words: "Therefore . . . be ye steadfast, immoveable, always abounding in the work of the Lord. . . ." See how practical it all is? And if you don't think it is practical, then I start reading I Corinthians 16: "Now concerning the collection. . . ." Now that's practicality.

It's as though Paul said, "There's a resurrection coming. Now will the ushers please come forward!" And really, it's all tied in. The people who are not thinking about the resurrection are not giving their tithes and offerings either. People who are not thinking about the coming of the Lord have forgotten that a final day is approaching; so they are laying up treasures on earth instead of in the bank of heaven.

But let's get back to the prophets. They make that same identical point with regard to motivating our lives toward holiness.

How should we interpret their predictive prophecies? In the interpretation of future events, there are two things that should be mentioned (but these are not a total hermeneutic). And perhaps these two things are where we run into the problem, more than anything else, of interpreting their future predictions.

The first item is the fulfillment of prophecy. How can we tell in what manner the fulfillment will come? Take, for example, things that the prophet spoke about that are still future to us. Perhaps Jesus' word in John 13:19 and 14:29 should help us.

Jesus didn't say, "I have told you these things before they come to pass so that when they do come to pass you might know that someone is right!" That's not what He said at all. Nor did

He say, "So that when it does come to pass you may know that a certain chart was right." What He did say was, "So that when it does come to pass *you may know that I am He.*" Prophecy is always a vindication of His Word and of His Person.

Then too, we must remember that there is a corollary to all this. History is always the final interpreter of prophecy. So that when it does come to pass you may know. Now that doesn't mean that I am totally in the dark. There are many things that I know accurately, but I don't know them comprehensively. And because I don't know comprehensively, I speak in pieces and I prophesy in pieces (I Cor. 13:12). I must always remember that I know in part and that I prophesy in part until He who is the completeness is come. Then the pieces will be put together, and the whole thing will fall into place.

So, interpretation of prophecy is always a study of Jesus and His great acts in history. Further history, and the actual happenings themselves, will reveal to us the fine details of interpretation. But then there is another issue in hermeneutics. It is the matter of conditionality. Is there such a thing as a condition that is to be observed in these prophecies? I think so. Read Jeremiah 18. Here is the account of the potter's house. Jeremiah was told to go down to the potter's house, and there he noticed that the potter was working on the wheel. However, as we read in verse 4, the vessel that the potter was making was marred in his hands. What did the potter do? He simply made it again.

Why was it marred? It could have been any number of things. There could have been a grain of sand in it. It could have been that the consistency of the clay was not right. Or it could have been that there was too little clay and too much sand. At any rate, by the time he got to the finishing part, something happened. The vessel was marred.

I think that the marring here can best be explained in terms of man's freedom. But how can it be "made again"? And according to what principle? The principle is announced in verses 7 to 10. Too often, we've used this passage only to demonstrate the sovereignty of God, which is there, of course. But we also need to see in this sovereignty passage, as in any other passage where you find that great theme, that human freedom is taught simultaneously.

I recommend Romans 9 to you. This is a great chapter emphasizing the sovereignty of God, and it is put side by side with another great chapter, Romans 10, which is the missionary chapter. They're back to back. Imagine that. The Lord must want us to talk to each other—the "sovereignty" people and the "freedom" people! Then in John 6, where we have a great passage on God's election of people, many of His disciples were offended when they heard it. "From that time many of his disciples went back, and walked no more with him."

But in the same chapter, Jesus said, "everyone that believeth, and everyone that cometh." Do you see the freedom there? In this passage of John they are also put side by side.

Thus back in Jeremiah 18:7-10, God explained to Jeremiah the principle by which He worked:

> At what instant I shall speak concerning a nation, and concerning a kingdom, to pluck up, and to pull down, and to destroy it; if that nation, against whom I have pronounced, turn from their evil, I will repent of the evil that I thought to do unto them, And at what instant I shall speak concerning a nation, and concerning a kingdom, to build and to plant it; if it do evil in my sight, that it obey not my voice, then I will repent of the good, wherewith I said I would benefit them.

See how God responds to men? And note that there is a conditionality there. This should also help to explain the Book of Jonah. Jonah knew what God would do; that's why he wanted to back out and run away. He said, in effect, "I know there is a conditionality to it. If I go up there and tell them judgment is coming in forty days and forty nights, and they repent, I know that You are a loving God, merciful and longsuffering, who will turn around. You won't bring judgment, I know You won't." Jonah is one of the books that explicates this principle of conditional prophecy.

Then someone says, "Well, that only happens with nations." But it happens with men, too. Look at I Kings 21. There we have that awful scene with Jezebel. In verse 4, we find Ahab pouting. Jezebel comes in and says, "What's the matter, honey?"

Ahab is acting like a spoiled child, and says, "Oh, it's that beautiful vineyard I see out my window. I'd like to have that. But Naboth owns it, and I know the Law of the Lord says I can't have it. It's just no use."

Then Jezebel says, "What's wrong with you? Are you a man or not? Who's king around here? Do you want the vineyard or don't you?"

"I want it all right, but it's no use," and Ahab continued pouting. Jezebel was a woman of determination and means. She hired two men, trumped up a charge, got Naboth in trouble, and had him put out of the way. Then she took over the field and soon came back to Ahab and said, "Now, that wasn't so hard at all was it?" Ahab had a little more perception, and he said, "Oh, no! You have no idea of the trouble you got me into now."

And he was so right. Soon, along came Elijah the Tishbite. Now Elijah was not the most sympathetic and patient man in the world. One gets the impression that he had suffered the rigors of a hard life, and when he spoke, he told it like it was. He was told by the Lord, in verse 18, to rise and go meet Ahab, the king of Israel, who has taken Naboth's vineyard. The Lord said, "I want you to tell him, 'Thus saith the Lord. In the place where dogs licked the blood of Naboth shall the dogs lick thy blood, even thine.' "

Ahab listened and then replied to Elijah, "Hast thou found me, O mine enemy? And he answered, I have found thee: because thou hast sold thyself to work evil in the sight of the Lord. Behold, I will bring evil upon thee, and will take away thy posterity, and will cut off from Ahab [all the male children], and him that is shut up and left in Israel, and I will make thine house like the house of Jeroboam the son of Nebat, and like the house of Baasha the son of Ahijah, for the provocation wherewith thou hast provoked me to anger, and made Israel to sin. And of Jezebel also spake the Lord, saying, The dogs shall eat Jezebel by the wall of Jezreel. Him that dieth of Ahab in the city the dogs shall eat; and him that dieth in the field shall the fowls of the air eat. But there was none like unto Ahab, which did sell himself to work wickedness in the sight of the Lord, whom Jezebel stirred up."

So what happened? In verse 27 we read, ". . . When Ahab heard those words . . . he rent his clothes, and put sackcloth upon his flesh, and fasted, and lay in sackcloth, and went softly." He plainly repented. And, then, in verse 29, God said: "Seest thou how Ahab humbleth himself before me? Because he humbleth himself before me, I will not bring the evil in his days: but in his son's days will I bring the evil upon his house."

Ahab repented, and God gave him a reprieve. "But," you say,

"his children suffered." But they suffered only because they were evil by their own decision. They would have never received the judgment, and the same conditionality would have been open to them, if they had responded to God the same way.

See how the Lord works on this principle? It operates for nations and for individuals as well. We preach the prophecy of what is going to take place, because the Word of the Lord is sure. But always remember that there is a suppressed "unless," a big "if." "Unless" we turn from the evil and the way in which we are walking.

God always has two options for men. Let me refer to the grandest prophecy of all as an example. It is found in Isaiah 19. In that passage, there is the case in which God says He is going to bring Israel back again to Himself. God will conclude history as He began it. It's a philosophy of history, as well as a hermeneutic of the prophets. And God dares to say that Egypt will also be brought back, along with Israel. And He does it in one of the most dramatic prophecies I know of in the Bible, where it speaks of Egypt going through economic disasters, political disasters, and finally sociological revolution. Perhaps we, today, are again right up near to the events forecasted in Isaiah 19. And what is the end of the prophecy? Does God only love Jewish people? No, never! He loves both Arabs and Jews, and they will end up going to the house of the Lord together. What a beautiful chapter!

Imagine! God speaks of the Egyptians, calling them "My people," the very phrase that He had used of Israel. But He doesn't stop there. He says to the Assyrians, the people who are now in Iraq and in present-day Syria, that they too shall come to the Lord's house to worship. And the Iraqi and the Egyptian and the Israeli shall be thirds in the house of the Lord. Now I ask you, have you ever seen that? Such grace! Such love! Such mystery! Do you know of any place in history where that has happened? These are the same nations that are on the scene today, and have been since 1948. God will yet fulfill His Word.

We could have debated that prophecy about a national restoration of Israel, prior to 1948. But now it is being fulfilled. The tremendous things that are rocking the Near East, even in our day, signify a build-up to this fulfillment. History will have to be the final revealer of that statement. But God says that Arabs,

Egyptians, and Jews shall go and worship Him together. And His Word is true.

That's just a sample as to the long range of prophecy. But it's not the only message. I give that just as a prime example of what the prophets said, and how there is still a message to God's people that speaks even to us and our day.

So much for the prophets and their message of righteousness and justice. We could have considered the social justice aspect as well, but it's there for the careful reader to see. Look at Isaiah 58 and see how he speaks for all social justice. It, too, gathers up the tangled skein of contemporary events of racial discrimination, poverty, ignorance, and oppression (Isa. 58:5-8). The prophets spoke to their day; they speak to our day; and they speak to a coming day, when we shall say:

"Then shall thy light break forth as the morning, and thine health shall spring forth speedily: and thy righteousness shall go before thee; the glory of the Lord shall be thy rereward" (Isa. 58:8).

# The Wisdom Books

## The Meaning of Life

In this chapter we shall be looking at one of the portions of the Old Testament that probably is both best known and least known. This is the section known as the Wisdom Literature: Psalms, Proverbs, Ecclesiastes, and Song of Solomon. We will bypass the Book of Psalms, since that is the section with which we are the most familiar. And although there are still some problems in that song book, particularly with the imprecatory Psalms, they must be left for a future discussion.[1]

So our discussion will be based on some verses that are found in Ecclesiastes, the book of "The Preacher." This is one of the greatest of the Wisdom Books. But before we look at that book, we should find out who these "wise men" are, who are mentioned in the Old Testament Wisdom Literature.

There are three classes of people found in Israel, as recorded in the Old Testament. One group is the priests of the Pentateuch. The second is the prophets whom we have discussed in a previous chapter. And there also is a class called "the wise men."

In Jeremiah there is a passage that ties the Historical Books to the Wisdom Books. We read in Jeremiah 8:5-9:

> Why then is this people of Jerusalem slidden back by a perpetual backsliding? They hold fast to deceit, they refuse to return. I hearkened and heard, but they spake not aright: no man repented him of his wickedness, saying, What have I done? every one turned to his course, as the horse rusheth into the battle. Yea, the stork in heaven

---

1. One of the best essays on this topic is by Chalmers Martin, "Imprecations in the Psalms" in *Classical Evangelical Essays in Old Testament Interpretation,* ed. Walter C. Kaiser, Jr. (Grand Rapids: Baker Book House, 1972), pp. 113-32.

knoweth her appointed times; and the turtle and the crane and the swallow observe the time of their coming; but my people know not the judgment of the Lord. How do ye say, *we are wise,* and the law of the Lord is with us? Lo, certainly in vain made he it; the pen of the scribes is in vain. *The wise men are ashamed,* they are dismayed and taken: lo, they have rejected the word of the Lord; *and what wisdom is in them?* (italics mine).

Then Jeremiah goes on to say at the end of verse 10:

. . . for every one from the least even unto the greatest is given to covetousness, from the prophet even unto the priest every one dealeth falsely. For they have healed the hurt of the daughter of my people slightly, saying peace, peace; when there is no peace. Were they ashamed when they had committed abomination? Nay, they were not at all ashamed, neither could they blush: therefore they shall fall among them that fall . . . (10-12).

What did the prophet say? In the strongest terms, he said that *possession* of the Word of God is nothing at all compared to the *response* to that Word of God. God's irrational creatures, like the birds of heaven (vs. 7) fly south when it comes time, when cold weather sets in. Can you imagine that? Every year they migrate. Rarely is there a holdout. There is no record of a flock of birds protesting, saying, "We refuse to take that long trip south. It's just a nuisance. Why should we observe the ordinances of God? Let's stay here in the cold north!" No, they don't act like that. God's irrational creatures respond to a built-in instinct.

Then what about God's rational creatures, the ones to whom He gave brains and common sense? Don't they know that the judgment of God is coming? Can't they smell it in the air? Don't they know that God is going to act, and fearful consequences will follow? "No," they say, "It will never come." So-called rational people keep whistling, walking right through the graveyard events of life, saying, "It can't happen here."

God appointed three types of leaders. And even they themselves are startled at the events. Some of these leaders were good; some of them were bad, or "false." There were the priests, then the prophets (some indeed were false prophets), and then there were the wise men. In our usual study of the Old Testament we have stressed the priests of the Law, and we have stressed the prophets of the prophecies, but perhaps we have not recognized this third category, the "wise men." In fact, in Ezekiel 7:26, Jeremiah 8:8-9, and 18:18, we see the prophets, the priests, and the wise men all being rebuked simultaneously for their failure in doing God's service. It is well known that the "wise man" of the Old Testament becomes the "scribe" of the New Testament. There also developed a group of scribes who later became the *Sopherim,* whom we see later in the Christian era, probably developing into the Massoretes, or at least one branch of them, who were responsible for giving us the so-called Massoretic text, with the vowels inserted in the traditional consonantal Hebrew text.

Moreover, this third class in Israel also seems to be part of an international guild. That the wise man is one of the three great classes of Israel is not the only point to be observed. It is also to be noted that there existed an international guild of wisdom according to the Bible. We have learned of the existence of such an international guild from the Near East, from Egyptian, Canaanite, Assyrian, and Babylonian literature. There are also many wisdom poems from Sumerian literature that could be classified with this group.

For example, the Biblical text itself comments on the wisdom of Edom in Obadiah, verse 7. Incidentally, the whole book is addressed to Edomites, a foreign nation. God even dares to repeat parts of Obadiah in Jeremiah 49, where He talks about the wisdom of the Edomites, that comes as a gift from God. Perhaps one of the men in Job 2:11 was a man who hailed from Edomite territory.

Then there is a reference to the wisdom of Tyre, as found in Ezekiel 27 and 28. There the prophet says that Tyre is really sitting in the shade; things have gone so easily for them. They have such tremendous commercial enterprises under way, their prosperity illustrating the wisdom of those people. The fantastic list of imports in Ezekiel 27 alone is a staggering indication of applied wisdom.

Again, the wisdom of Egypt is referred to in Genesis 41, where the people were clever enough to follow Joseph's wise leadership and thus preserve their nation. In Exodus 7 we read of the magicians who were clever enough to counterfeit the first two plagues at least. And the wisdom of Egypt in former days is referred to in Isaiah 19:11-15.

Even Solomon is said to have been wiser than both the sons of the East, the *Bene qedem,* and the children who came from Egypt. Solomon was even wiser than all these men (cf. I Kings 4:30).

But the Bible is nothing if it is not an open and an honest book. It takes note that there are also pagan, godless people who have wisdom. And it continues by recording the wisdom of Babylon, in Isaiah 44 and Jeremiah 50 and 51. The wisdom of Persia is referred to in Esther 1:13. And there are many, many other Biblical references. In other words, the Bible shows that wisdom in and for itself is not something that belongs to a select club. It comes from the living God Himself. This is part of the common grace of God that is given out to all men. And the Bible reflects this.

Well, so much for the "International Wisdom Guild." What about wisdom in the Biblical text itself? Wisdom as a revelation from God? The Bible, ever logical, gives us, first of all, the promise in the Pentateuch, the promise doctrine that we traced out in chapter two. Then the Bible adds to the promise, a further amplification of the law as being the means by which that promise can be carried out in the lives of those who are redeemed. Bible study takes us on into the Prophets, who are *preachers* of the law and *announcers* of that promise theme. Then we move into the Wisdom area of the Bible.

How does the Wisdom Literature function? Unfortunately, many theologians drop out here and do not know what to do with this wisdom material. Some say, "Oh, those are just slogans, mottoes to hang up on the wall. Or perhaps they are good instructions for parents to give to the children. It might help keep young people in line—to give them a verse from Proverbs!"

But this is not what Wisdom Literature is all about. It's more than that. The Wisdom Literature commends the truth that the Law has commanded. What the Law specifies is repeated in the Wisdom Books. Fortunately, many evangelicals who cannot accept the Law are, interestingly enough, exposing their hand. They do not seem to realize that when they go to the Wisdom Books they are establishing the same things that the Law provided. In the Wisdom Literature, however, they are given in proverbial and in universally abiding terms. There is so much wisdom woven into the format of the Wisdom Literature, but its stimulus is the revealed Law of God. Just as the prophets were mainly announcers of the promise theme and incidentally preachers of the Law, so the Wisdom writers are primarily teachers of the Law and only in a lesser way explainers of the promise doctrine. When we look for the principle behind the Wisdom Literature, we find the moral Law of God. It is actually a return to the Law of God. As Deuteronomy preaches the Law, the Wisdom Books put it into short, understandable phrases that are both quotable and easily digested.

A wisdom literary device, such as a proverb, is something that is terse, brief, has a little "kick" to it, and has a little bit of salt as well. Take a little bit of kick, a little bit of salt, and some brevity; mix them with God-given (or in the case of Scripture— with some revelatory) ability, and you've got a proverb. But what lies behind the proverb? Well, if you were to write it out in a prose sentence, you would no doubt be casting it in the form as it appeared in the Law of Moses!

However we accept or use the Wisdom Literature, there is in it the union of "the right" in terms of the Law, and the "righteous God" who commands it. Furthermore, wisdom is the cure for one of the greatest diseases of religion—a lack of reality, or unreality. This has been heard widely in the Christian community lately. It is time that we turned back to the Wisdom Books. They show us how life is and how it should be lived. It demonstrates how to be real, identifiable, and meaningful.

Some people get a flabby, stuffy, indoor, hot-house quality to their Christian experience. They seem to be afraid of the big, wide outdoors. Then they complain about the lack of reality in others and in the Church. Are they afraid that hiding somewhere is a big, bad religious liberal with loads of soul-destroying facts? They're afraid that he is really in the weeds, waiting for that flabby, indoor Christian to walk by. And as he walks by, out pops the liberal saying, "Boo! I've got you!"

Does the flabby Christian stand there, teeth chattering, startled, and completely disarmed? Or does he make it back to his church as fast as he can, seal himself in that citadel, and promise his Lord never to go out into the world again or study another secular fact? Does he conclude that there's the world and here is the church and never the twain shall meet?

Well, the Wisdom Literature dares to come out into the market-place. Wisdom as you know, is out in the streets—in the shopping plazas and universities. We read that she calls to all that pass by, and offers wisdom to all people, if only they will receive it.

But how does one get wisdom? By finishing a degree? No! The Bible says it starts with "the fear of the Lord." And the fear of the Lord is not something that makes one's teeth chatter. It is not something that makes a person bite his fingernails, saying, "I w-w-wonder what's going to happen?" It isn't a question of, "I wonder if this really is for me?" The fear of the Lord is a stance. It is an attitude of the heart. It is something that places an individual in a proper relationship with God. It speaks of His fellowship.

As a matter of fact, "the fear of the Lord" is probably the only word in the Old Testament for "religion." There does not seem to be another word for religion. Also, there is not a word for "theology." What we do find in its place, is probably the Old Testament word for "the knowledge of God." So the word for religion in the Old Testament is probably "fear of the Lord."

In the Bible, the fear of the Lord is worked out in terms of a man's attitude. It is one in which his whole sense of life is openness to the living God. That is the beginning of everything. It is the beginning of living. Moreover, Wisdom Literature tells us that there is singularity to God's work. This is God's *uni*verse, or "one verse." People used to be able to sing one song, one verse, because they had the one Lord who made the one verse—who made the one world, *the uni verse.* So any topic, any subject studied would follow and flow into an integrated meaning of life, because the Lord God had made it such. That's where the word *university* came from. It is unfortunate that the university has lost its original concept, and is now a multiversity at its best.

The big question now is, "Where can I find that oneness?" Go back to the Wisdom Books and the revelation of God. For the Bible says, ". . . in wisdom hast thou made them all" (Ps. 104:24). So I begin to see the oneness in God's works.

Moreover, in the Wisdom Books, we see the meaningfulness of God's world. We read in Psalm 111:2, "The works of the Lord are great." The text goes on, "sought out of all those that have pleasure therein." And so there is a mandate, an openness to all that God has. Some people take time out, and seek to study all of God's works. Unfortunately, many go off on tangents that lead them away from God, His wisdom, and His revelation.

Beyond this, the Wisdom Books tell us that man is built with a hunger to know the integration of all things. Here's where the Book of Ecclesiastes can help us to see the wonderful unity of all things. I myself am unfulfilled, not only as a Christian, but as a man, a man made in the image of God, until I understand how everything fits together in this world. I am terribly, insatiably curious. But did you know something? The Bible says I was built that way. The men over at the university were built that way. Everyone is built that way. And I say this on the basis of the Word of God.

Let's examine the Book of Ecclesiastes and find out what it is trying to teach.

Canon J. Stafford Wright has written beautifully about this book.[2] He said that there are three things to do when studying a book. First of all, you can look at the preface, or the introduction, and ask what the author proposes to do in his work. What does he want to accomplish in this work? The preface of Ecclesiastes says, "Vanity of vanities, saith the Preacher, vanity of vanities; all is vanity." Briefly translated, he seems to say, "life is one big zero." It's not worth bothering about. It sounds like one of Winnie-the-Pooh's characters, Eeyore, who constantly says, "Oh bother, bother." Indeed, the word "vanity" is the kind of thing you see on a cold morning when you open up your mouth and exhale. It is the vapor that comes out. It's there and it's gone. Does he mean that life is transient—here now but then gone so quickly?

"Vanity of vanities" does not seem to immediately give us a clue to the purpose of the book. We really do not know whether the writer is saying that everything is futile, that everything is empty and nothing is worth living for. That certainly has a very pessimistic ring. That is precisely where we are with regard to modern culture. If I understand where the arts are going, in their *avant garde* leadership in society, and if we are not being led astray, then they seem to be saying, it's all over.

Are you familiar with Samuel Beckett's work, particularly his

---

2. He has kindly allowed me to reproduce his study on this book in its entirety. See Canon J. Stafford Wright, "The Interpretation of Ecclesiastes" in *Classical Essays,* ibid., pp. 133-50.

play, "Waiting for Godot"? The lines are very simple and extremely repetitious. One tramp says, "What are you doing here?" The other says, "We're waiting."

"Who are we waiting for?"

"We're waiting for Godot."

They go over and over that again for two hours, until you could go mad. And who is Godot? Well, it is probably a French diminutive form for God. As I take it, that's what he's getting at. They are waiting for God, waiting for something to happen.

That was Beckett away back in 1952 (the French play was translated into English in 1954). He now has a long string of credits to his name. Several years ago, one of his most recent plays was staged for television viewing and for discussion. What was it? The curtain opened. In the middle of the stage was a whole pile of junk, obviously just litter and pollution all over the place. There was not one human being in the cast. They were not needed any more. There was the wail of a baby offstage. Then silence. Then you heard the groan of a man. Then the curtain closed.

They could have run that play over and over several times during one evening's performance. And they did. They did it over again. Then it was discussed. It was an eloquent statement on modern man. Man has disappeared from the scene. Junk is all that's left. And what is on the other side of the junk pile? Birth (the baby) and death (the groans of the man). Nothing else is left.

If there ever was a day in which to preach the gospel, this is it. That's what the "vanity" of Ecclesiastes is all about. Man is in bad shape. And he knows it. He knows he's in bad shape. So I must tell modern man of One who is able to help him. What must he do? That's where this Wisdom of God is needed. "The fear of the Lord is the beginning" of that wisdom.

Let us return to our analysis of Ecclesiastes. We were mentioning three ways in which we could study a book. The first way, that of examining the preface, does not seem to be too promising in this case. How do you usually read a book? Some people play fair; they read the preface, then proceed through the book to its conclusion. But there are some who cannot wait, particularly if they are reading a mystery story. How does it turn out? "Whodunit?" And so they cheat a little and read the conclusion first. The Book of Ecclesiastes also is a book of mystery—the mystery of life or the mystery of wisdom for life. In Ecclesiastes 12:13 and 14, it says: "Let us hear the conclusion of the whole matter." The writer, the preacher has said "Vanity, vanity, vanity, vanity," thirty-seven times. (It's only used in all of the other thirty-eight books of the Old Testament, thirty-three times!) He adds it all up, and gets zero—a big, egg-shaped zero!

Now, even the simplest of mathematicians knows that when you add zero to zero, $0+0+0+0$, even to infinity, it still comes to zero. But the full text of Ecclesiastes 12:13 is, "Let us hear the conclusion of the whole matter: Fear God and keep his commandments: for this is the whole duty of man." Notice that the word "duty" isn't in the original Hebrew text. It is not just a *duty* to fear God and keep His commandments. It is what man was created for, bringing the totality of life into subjection to His will. And only sin mars its fulfillment.

The Preacher goes on: "For God shall bring every work into judgment, with every secret thing, whether it be good, or whether it be evil." Thus concludes this book of wisdom.

How did he ever get to that conclusion? Some scholars can't believe it, so they say that it's a late addition to the original pessimistic version or this has been added to the text later on. They really can't see that it belongs there. But it is there alright, in the Hebrew manuscript. Hear the conclusion of the matter. For that is where the writer is taking us. "Fear God, and keep his commandments, for this is the whole duty ('mannishness') of man." Do you want to know what a man is? Here it is. He is an eternal, ongoing creation of God. And then we read that God "shall bring every work [of man] into judgment. . . ." All man's work into judgment? But earlier the book said that when you're dead, you're dead—just like the animals. So who worries about a judgment if that is true?

". . . with every secret thing, whether it be good . . . or evil." Why should this concern us? For a very good reason! And that reason is given to us even more clearly in the New Testament. Paul has written of this, for example, in II Corinthians 5:10, "For we must all appear before the judgment seat of Christ; that every one may receive the things done in his body, whether . . . good or bad." And Paul doubtless got his teaching from God through this Wisdom passage in Ecclesiastes.

Nevertheless, even though we have looked at the preface and

then the conclusion, there are still many problems in this book. It is the body of Ecclesiastes that carries the main themes, and several of them are repeated for emphasis. And this is the third method of studying a book. What are these themes that keep recurring throughout the book? Perhaps you've read the book already, and have some answers. You have noticed references to an Epicurean-like phrase that says, "Eat, drink and be merry, for tomorrow we die." That theme recurs several times. Many people say that these Epicurean refrains are in line with the total pessimism of the book. But look at them again. For instance, in Ecclesiastes 2:24, "There is nothing better for man, than that he should eat and drink, and that he should make his soul enjoy good in his labour. . . ." If a period is placed there, and the sentence concluded, you do have pessimism. But notice that the text goes on to say, in fulfilling the grammatical idea, ". . . This also I saw, that it was from the hand of God." What was from the hand of God? Did God provide for eating, drinking, and making your soul enjoy the good of your labor? Someone will argue that God is not interested in such things. He wants my soul. He's not interested in my material, physical being. Or is He? The text says, ". . . this also I saw, that it was from the hand of God."

The Bible is replete with God's concern for man's total being. The secular aspect of life cannot be cut off from the sacred aspects of life. Even though one is tainted strongly with sin, it still was originally made by God, is presently being used by Him, and will one day be perfectly restored to Him. So away with this horrible, unscriptural bifurcation.

Notice another emphasis along this line, in chapter 3:12-13: "I know that there is no good in them, but for a man to rejoice, and to do good in his life. And also that every man should eat and drink, and enjoy the good of his labour . . ."—what follows, a period? No, there is a comma and an additional phrase: "it is the gift of God." God provides these things, too.

Or look at chapter 3:22: "Wherefore I perceive that there is nothing better, than that a man should rejoice in his own works; for that is his portion [that is what he is here for]: for who shall bring him to see what shall be after him?" Evidently people say, "I guess no one will review things after the end, at least I wouldn't." Remember, however, the conclusion that we looked at ahead of time: "God shall bring every work into judgment" (12:14.) Therefore the question in 3:22 is rhetorical. It sets us up for the solution to just such a silly thought, that there will be no review.

Then read chapter 5:18 and 19, "Behold that which I have seen: it is good and comely for one to eat and to drink, and to enjoy the good of his labour that he taketh under the sun all the days of his life . . ."—again, do we find a period? How uselessly laborious if that is the end. No, read on—". . . which God giveth him: for it is his portion."

And in chapter 8:15, we have another so-called Epicurean phrase. "Then I commended mirth, because a man hath no better thing under the sun, than to eat, and to drink, and to be merry: for that shall abide with him of his labour the days of his life . . ." —and again God is in it, as we read—". . . which God giveth him under the sun."

Do you see where these themes carry us? Life and all it means is not simply eating, drinking, laughing, making love, and then the end. God is in them all! Or He wants to be.

Turn to chapter 9:7 ff. and see how God enters all of life. "Go thy way, eat thy bread with joy, and drink thy wine with a merry heart; for God now accepteth thy works. Let thy garments be always white; and let thy head lack no ointment. Live joyfully with the wife whom thou lovest all the days of the life of thy vanity, which he hath given thee under the sun, all the days of thy vanity. . . ." How about that! Life, and all the pleasures of life. Eating and drinking, the very clothes that we wear; marriage and the marriage bed; family and all its joys—these all come from God and are under the scrutiny of God. Wisdom indeed! These are all gifts of God.

Can you see how wide and broad the Biblical revelation is? It's not just the bringing of man into a relationship with Jesus Christ, although that is central and primary. But man in his total being, along with his world and every area of his life, belongs to the living God. If these refrains formerly seemed to be Epicurean, instead, they now suddenly turn out to be something of a verdict on all of life.

To recapitulate, let us go back to the idea of the preface. In Ecclesiastes, thirty-seven times the word *vanity* is repeated. There are also seventy-one separate topics, which a noted Bible scholar has listed in this area. He lists not only seventy-one topics, but emphasizes that God's name occurs forty times in Ecclesiastes, particularly twelve times when the thought shows that God gives all these good gifts from His hand. We are also reminded that "under the sun" appears twenty-eight times.

How then should we understand the preface? What must we think when we read "vanity of vanities, all is vanity"? There is one little clue, the key verse in the book, which is chapter 3:11: "He hath made everything beautiful in its time: also he hath set [eternity] in their heart, so that no man can find out the work that God maketh from the beginning to the end." In the KJV, it reads: "He hath set *the world* in their heart." I don't know why they translated the word as "the world." Certainly their marginal reading is to be preferred, so that it correctly says: "He hath set *eternity* in their heart, so that no man can find out the work that God maketh from the beginning to the end."

What is the writer saying? I, like everyone else, am hungry to know how everything fits together. God has built me that way. I want to know the eternity of everything. I want to know how the arts, sciences, and humanities fit together with theology, and how they all fit together with the plan of God. Because God does have a plan, not only for Himself, but for me, for you. Eating and drinking are part of that plan, too, as we have seen. I do not want to be involved in them if they do not fit into the plan of God. I do not want to be involved in marriage if it doesn't fit within the plan of God. Indeed, all the issues of my life must come under His scrutiny and His control. I find that God has a plan for individuals that involves the entirety of life.

But when we come back to this phrase "vanity of vanities," the writer is not saying that all is ultimately emptiness, that nothing is worth living for. What he is saying is that life *in and of itself* is not able to give the key that unlocks its treasures. What is the key to life? Don't go to university and ask the university to open up life with just one subject, one discipline. Don't think that philosophy is the key. Don't think that science will unlock it. Don't think that theology is it. As a matter of fact, Ecclesiastes runs through each of these themes, and you can find them all, and then says: "This won't do; this just won't do." None of them will fit the lock of man's empty heart *unless* he first comes to put his full trust in the living God and His Word. Only then will he be able to see how positively thrilling all of life, study, and working really is.

In Ecclesiastes 1:4-9, we have a graphic picture of nature. Perhaps you have watched the sun set on a beautiful lake. Or you've been stirred as you have seen the Rockies, or some other of the great panoramas of nature. But what does all this really add up to? Again, zero. Vanity. Because whereas there are pleasures in seeing them, they will not give you the "wholeness" and "wholesomeness" of life. They will not give you the wholeness of what man is made for. That is reserved for man meeting God. The knowledge of the Lord is the beginning of wisdom.

Perhaps you think wisdom itself is the answer. Then Ecclesiastes 1:13 says, "You may try that for the key to life." You can think, this is it, this will unlock everything for me. Go ahead. Try a little bit of wisdom. You will find out that of the making of books, and much else that comes under the guise of wisdom, there is no end (cf. 12:12). And you will find yourself distressed, because the more you know, the more you find you don't know. And that's terribly humiliating. It's helpful, but it's also maddening. So you can't use wisdom for the ultimate key either.

What else is there? You may try a little pleasure. Or as Ecclesiastes says, "I will turn to folly" (2:12). But that's only going to lead in the opposite direction. It's far better to get wisdom than folly. So that's not the key either.

Thus the preacher takes us through the whole book, saying, "I tried this. . . . I tried this. . . . I tried this. . . ." Actually he says that no one thing in all of this world will provide the key or meaning to life. Not one! Most of them are good. They are gifts from God. They can be helpful. But there is no true wisdom until you come to know the One who gave you all these things. "The fear of the Lord is the beginning of wisdom" (Prov. 9:10).

The fear of the Lord is also the beginning of pleasure. The fear of the Lord is the true beginning of marriage. The fear of the Lord is the only beginning of living. The fear of the Lord is the beginning of eating. The fear of the Lord is the beginning of drinking. These are not just cliches. These are for men, because God built them that way. If we want to understand how God built a man or a woman, and how they can find their own fullness of life, listen to God's plan. And that is certainly what He is saying here.

Some people are so desperate that they even try death. They turn to death in seeking for the key. Others are perplexed by the reference of Ecclesiastes 3:18: "I said in mine heart concerning the estate of the sons of men, that God might manifest them, and that they might see that they themselves are beasts."

And they tell us to also look at 3:19, "For that which befalleth the sons of men befalleth beasts; even one thing befalleth them: as the one dieth, so dieth the other; yea, they all have one breath; so that a man hath no preeminence above a beast; for all is vanity. All go unto one place; all are of the dust, and all turn to dust again."

Is that the end? Is it a vicious circle without meaning or purpose? But this is the natural man reasoning. That's not the Biblical man.

Then why would God take twelve chapters to tell us how a natural man reasons, and only give us two verses on the end, that say, "Don't forget, fear the Lord, keep His commandments, for this is the whole of man"? It seems that such a pessimistic interpretation of Ecclesiastes is really giving too much visibility to the other side. And it's not even being fair, because throughout the book, as we have seen, there are these other themes that show the activity of God.

Look again at chapter 3:18-22, and then move along to 8:17 and read, ". . . I beheld all the work of God, that a man cannot find out the work that is done under the sun. . . ." Then proceed down to 9:4, "For to him that is joined to all the living there is hope; for a living dog is better than a dead lion. For the living know that they shall die: but the dead know not any thing, neither have they any more a reward; for the memory of them is forgotten." If the writer's conclusion is so pessimistic as people allege, then who cares for either living or dying? And that's our point. It wasn't pessimism! Nor was life dull! Nor was the grave the end of it all! They were told that judgment was coming. As a matter of fact, that's the conclusion of the whole thing; "For God shall bring every work into judgment." If a man really thought that death ended all, he wouldn't care about the future. But the writer does care, as we see, and he also wants all men everywhere to care for the same reasons.

What is the point of this passage, and the one in chapter 11:8 ff? Listen to it: "But if a man live many years, and rejoice in them all; yet let him remember the days of darkness; for they shall be many. All that cometh is vanity." My understanding of these particular passages that deal with death, is that the writer is saying: "while you've got life, don't just sit there. Do something! Do something for the glory of God! Don't you understand that there is a divine plan now, a divine inspection in the future? Don't you know that you have been given life and breath in this present world? That this is your last opportunity to work?"

There is a job for all, which can help to bring God's plan to fruition in this present period of history. Why should anyone sit by while there is life, a precious commodity to use wisely and carefully? Do something with it. Do something for the glory of God.

What we really have here is not a fatalistic or pessimistic view of a future life. The writer says that all animal life share two things: a physical body that goes to dust, and a life principle that is a gift from God, and that returns to Him. And it's never, never too late, as long as you are alive, to take part in God's plan.

You can know where you are going under the sun. The dead have run their course, and they await judgment. On the other hand, while it is yet day, do the works of Him who called you. Or, to borrow a phrase from John 9:4, "I must work the works of him that sent me, while it is day: the night cometh when no man can work."

In this life there are no guarantees of success under the sun. There is no infallible guidance for 100 percent proof of success. There is no promise of a life without hardships. On the other hand, God has a plan, and in Christ our fingers touch the very beginning of that plan. Having been given life, we have been given the greatest asset in the world.

So what does this "vanity of vanities, all is vanity" mean? I take it to mean that life is unable to give or be in itself, the key. See chapter 3:11 and 7:14. In this latter verse we read: "In the day of prosperity be joyful, but in the day of adversity consider: God also hath set the one over against the other, to the end that man should find nothing after him." There is nothing apart from God. Sometimes God increases our joy that we might know His fullness. Sometimes God decreases it and takes us into suffering, so that we have nothing else left but Him. Try to understand that when everything else passes away, only God is left.

In 8:17, the writer says, ". . . that a man cannot find out the work that is done under the sun: because though a man labour to seek it out, yet he shall not find it; yea further; though a wise man

129

think to know it, yet shall he not be able to find it." So where can it be found? Only in the revelation of the God who has spoken in the Scriptures! And when there is an attitude of openness to receive that Word, then we realize that "the fear of God is the beginning of wisdom."

All this leads to the conclusion. Look at the refrain in Ecclesiastes 12:13, "Let us hear the conclusion of the whole matter." We have seen that life in and of itself is unable to supply the key. To try this, or try that, or try the other thing, is useless. There is only one thing that can supply the key, only one Person. So hear the conclusion: "Fear God, and keep his commandments: for this is the whole duty of man. For God shall bring every work into judgment, with every secret thing, whether it be good or . . . evil" (Eccles. 12:13, 14).

Man by his very nature is a rebellious, troublesome creature. We see this in our very day. He wants to tear down society. The students come with a hunger for the integration of all things, hoping that someone is going to make them completely liberated men. They desire to be free from their provincialism. They want to receive a genuine liberal education, in the sense of a liberal arts education.

When present-day students, with this built-in hunger to know the eternity, the integration of all things, begin seeking, what happens? Someone starts telling them the mostest about the leastest. And the student says, I understand, I understand. I have memorized all the individual terms and facts. I understand everything about that butterfly wing that you told me. But what about the butterfly? What about the world that the butterfly flies in? What about me and butterflies? Won't you please tell me?

And the teacher says, "You'll have to get that in another class." But the other class is of no help either. They also tell the mostest about the leastest. And when does it all get put back together? The world seems to be coming apart; and what can be done about it?

The intellectuals say that there's not much that can be done ∟bout it. But the student has been stirred up, and says, "There is something I can do about it." What can he do? Live as immorally as he pleases! Or turn on to any drugs that he wants! But, comes the response, "You ought not to do that." And a belligerent question comes back: "What do you mean, I *ought* not to do that? Where did you get that phrase 'ought not'? You told me that that word is not valued any more. Everything is relative. So why not do anything that I please?"

There is something desperately wrong here. We say, "Don't destroy your life." But on what basis? And there is no concrete answer coming back. Only the evil in man's nature can find expression, and he does his own thing. This is what is developing in the Western Hemisphere. Watch it, and weep for the hopelessness of man.

Read Francis Schaeffer's book, *"The Church at the End of the Twentieth Century.* You will see the Book of Ecclesiastes come alive in the predicament of the twentieth century. Schaeffer affirms the certainty of a divine plan. God is going to bring every work into judgment. There is also the certainty that the Christian has a great opportunity to serve now in this body, while he has life. But it's a gift, God's gift.

Today is a surprise package, as is every day. There is no contract that says that you must have this day to live. It's a daily surprise. And God's mercies are "renewed every morning" to meet the surprises of each day.

We find more in the Wisdom Literature. There is beauty. In Ecclesiastes 3, there is a beauty to the quest for eternity that is in us. Whenever you see a person who longs to know the integration of all things, who longs to know how all this can fit together, but who pursues to fill this longing in the fear of God, that is the most beautiful thing, more beautiful even than any rigorous academic pursuits. The true meaning to life comes with the beginning of a relationship to the living God, who has manifested Himself in the promise, who has continued to tell us what He is in His Person and in His Nature in the Law, and who has given the emphasis of the priority within that Law through the prophets. He also commends it to us in practical ways and applies it to us in books like Ecclesiastes. Here is true wisdom.

We need one additional measure of Wisdom Literature, and that is the Song of Solomon.[3] The same truth applies here, as to Ecclesiastes. To find out what this book says, look at Song of Solo-

---

3. A much fuller development was given by J. Godet, "The Interpretation of the Song of Songs" in *Classical Evangelical Essays,* ibid., pp. 151-74. See the bibliography there on the Wisdom Literature, pp. 174-75.

mon 8:7, where we are told, "Many waters cannot quench love, neither can floods drown it: if a man would give all the substance of his house for love, it would utterly be condemned [despised]." And the verse before it says, "Set me as a seal upon thine heart, as a seal upon thine arms; for love is strong as death; jealousy is cruel as the grave; the coals thereof are coals of fire, which hath a most vehement flame." I think the translation should read, "which is as a flame of Jehovah," i.e., a flame of the Lord. God's name should be kept here in this particular section.

There is a theology of marriage taught in this book that is unparalleled in its excellence. I know of the relationship that exists between Christ and the Church, which is so beautifully taught in Ephesians. But in the Song of Songs God has shown marriage to be such a beautiful thing, and so important. He had already given the first instructions to man in the Garden of Eden on how he should treat his wife. Genesis speaks of what a beautiful relationship should exist between the two of them. It also comes out strongly in this song.

Song of Solomon tells us of a girl that Solomon tried to woo. But did so unsuccessfully—she would have none of him. There is a third character, who has not always been seen here. It is the shepherd boy who is portrayed as the girl's rustic lover back home. The girl and the boy apparently had an understanding before Solomon came along and saw her. She must have been quite a raving beauty to capture the king's attention so raptly.

The king decided that he must have this girl for his own. He took her back to the palace and tried to get her ready for the wedding. Meanwhile, the daughters of Jerusalem, who were part of Solomon's harem, kept talking to this girl and saying, "You are fortunate. You've got it made. Solomon can give you everything."

And she says, "I don't want everything. I want love. I want my boyfriend. I want to go back home."

Here is a very emotional, delicate, and tender book. Be careful how you read it. There may be some offense, because it speaks in terms of an oriental society, and its frank and endearing terms of body and spirit are from that culture. As you know, there are many variations that occur between cultures, concerning which parts of the body may be referred to in good public taste. For example, the neck was much more impressive to Easterners than it is to us. But the point is still to be made, that within the text there is a beautiful description of the girl herself, and even of the lover, and it is done with propriety and delicacy.

There is a theology of marriage that is offered here, one in which God says that the very love that is placed in a person is from the Lord God Himself. "And," says Solomon, as he writes this book and tells, under the inspiration of God, of his defeat, "many waters cannot quench love, neither can the floods drown it: if a man would give all the substance of his house for love, he would utterly be [despised]." He was learning a great lesson, the lesson of love and its value.

It seems to me that here is the most beautiful description of the marriage relationship that is to be found anywhere in literature. Our day and age is obsessed with sexology. The whole discussion of sex has been taken from its place of loveliness and beauty to be paraded to sell almost everything.

The enjoyments and beauty that God has placed *within* the marriage relationship were meant *for* the marriage relationship. As an evangelical and a believer in the Scriptures, I want that back again. I dare to affirm that that is part of the beauty of the Biblical teaching. It is part of that practical application of the Word of God, which began with the promise, went on with the Law, and was announced and preached by the Prophets. Now it is commended to us again, in a very delicate way.

God says that as you enter into marriage, as He gives you the gift for marriage and you receive it, preserve yourselves for one another.

In chapter 8:10, the girl talks once again in a very personal way about how she finds herself in relation to the bridegroom. In the last phrase she says, "Then was I in his eyes as one that found [peace]." It's translated in the KJV as "favour," but I think that the better English translation is that she was able to offer him "peace." The English "favour" hardly indicates the richness to be found here. *Shalom* is the experience of joy and purpose and peace. It is a sense of integration, not only between the sexes, but within the man himself and within the woman herself, and in relation to the world that God has made. Here is the consummation of the marriage of a pure woman with a good man as they give themselves completely to each other, body and soul. And as the Biblical text shows, God is interested in what a man and a woman do with their bodies.

This is part of the frankness and the delicacy seen in the Biblical text. And this is not only the will of the Lord for the marriage union, but also it shows the harmony that God built into human relationships at the beginning of the world.

Remember, however, that there is not only the Shulamite maiden here, the one who was brought before Solomon, but there is also the shepherd boy who is back home. In the last chapter of the Song of Solomon, she wins out, or rather love wins out, and she goes back home to her shepherd boy. Solomon states that he has observed that nothing—neither money nor a palace—can compete with real love, for it is given by God. And the maiden says finally, in verse 12, "My vineyard which is mine, is before me: thou, O Solomon, must have a thousand, and those that keep the fruit thereof, two hundred." Solomon, you have your many. I have only one. (Incidentally, there seems to be a condemnation here of Solomon's polygamous situation.) But the lesson is well learned when we see God's harmony in all of life. And He enters into every human experience to give meaning to life, and in Him we fulfill God's highest purpose: "The chief end of man is to glorify God, and enjoy Him forever" (Westminster Shorter Catechism).

# Conclusion

The Old Testament is not only a good complement to the New Testament, but it is also exciting evidence that the revelation of God comes through to the thoughtful reader. Perhaps we cannot understand everything. But may I challenge you to check out these nuggets of truth, and the many more that you can mine for yourself. Get into the text and enjoy reading it once again. You will find the Lord speaking to you here. The God of the universe who felt we were important enough to come and visit us in the Person of His only Son, has also thought it important enough to give us this system of meanings, and to communicate His values and judgments to us.

May we become a wise people, joyfully looking forward to our Lord, and His return. May we sense the certainty of His plan, and thank Him for the meaningfulness of life and the integration of all things. And let us ask Him that, while there still is life in our bones, He take us and use us for His glory. And may there come a great revival in our time, and a great reformation. Pray that God will do this, and ask Him how each one of us might fit His plan and purpose. The world needs Him badly. It needs us and our lives and witness. We serve the God of all eternity. We must understand this.